GOD, SEX & GENERATION X

Mike Starkey is vicar of a multicultural church in Finsbury Park, North London, and bestselling author of *Fashion & Style* and *Born to Shop* (Monarch).

A former commercial radio journalist, he regularly appears on national TV and radio. His TV appearances include *The Big Breakfast* and *Esther*, and he contributes to *New Christian Herald*, the *Church Times* and London's *Premier* Radio.

He is married to Naomi and they have two children, Joel and Joy.

Very best wishes,

Mike Starkey.

GOD, SEX & GENERATION X

A Search for Lost Wonder

MIKE STARKEY

TRIANGLE

First published in Great Britain in 1997
Triangle
SPCK
Holy Trinity Church
Marylebone Road
London NW1 4DU

British Library Cataloguing-in-Publication Data
A catalogue record of this book is available from
the British Library

ISBN 0-281-05009-0

Typeset by Pioneer Associates, Perthshire
Printed in Great Britain by
BPC Paperbacks Ltd.

for Naomi

CONTENTS

ACKNOWLEDGEMENTS

Most of the individuals cited by way of illustration have been disguised to avoid identification. In some cases the name, gender and other details have been changed; others are composites, made up of more than one real-life person.

Special thanks to Tom Smail, for his wise comments on an earlier version of the manuscript, and Rachel Boulding who edited it. Biggest thanks of all go to Naomi, to whom this book is dedicated. She not only provided the original impetus for the book, but its conclusions have grown largely out of our shared reflections and experiences together.

If *God, Sex & Generation X* moves just one person a fraction closer towards the Source of the wonder I have tried to evoke in these pages, it will have been worth it.

Mike Starkey
Finsbury Park, London

INTRODUCTION:
THE AWE IN ORDINARY

won+der n. 1. the feeling excited by something strange; a mixture of surprise, curiosity, and sometimes awe. **2.** something that causes such a feeling, such as a miracle.

Collins English Dictionary

LATE WITH THE NEWS

The first tentative hints of dawn were starting to appear in the dark sky. I gripped the wheel of the car, leaning forward, straining to see through the driving rain. My headlamps on full beam, my heart pounding even faster and more violently than the frantic windscreen wipers. I was late. Very late.

It was 5.30 am. We had stayed out till gone midnight the previous evening. A big mistake when you are working the early shift, especially when your vocal, new-born son robs you of even your few short hours of badly needed sleep. By 6.00 I had to be in the small, soundproofed booth, headphones on, fader up, with a calm voice which belied the chaos in newsreader and newsroom: *CNFM News at 6.00 am*.

In less than half-an-hour I had to achieve the impossible. Firstly, finish the drive along the winding country lanes between our isolated cottage and the radio station on the edge of Cambridge. Then unlock the station doors, make my way to the newsroom and check the overnight computer 'feed' of stories from Independent Radio News in London. Select and edit some 20-second pieces of audio from the overnight, automatic tape machine; phone the local emergency services; follow up any local

1

stories; write the local news; compile a three-minute bulletin of national, international and local news. And then be seated in the news booth, ready for the exact second when the long hand on the studio clock hits the vertical.

It would take a miracle. Or maybe just a little more speed. I pushed my foot down hard on the accelerator, confident that I could manoeuvre the car round each serpentine curve of the lanes I knew so well. I had not reckoned with the wet road, the dark sky, the blinding rain, the sheer fatigue which dulled my every reaction. Suddenly I found myself speeding round a bend which seemed sharper than I had ever remembered. Suddenly the car entered an uncontrollable skid, wildly careering from one side of the road to the other.

I had never enjoyed fairgrounds. Now I was in my very own white-knuckle ride, spinning out of control. I felt the car fly off the road, over a deep drainage ditch, and turn a somersault in mid-air. For those few seconds, the sense of powerlessness was overwhelming. 'O God,' I prayed. 'Help.'

The car, now in mid-somersault, bounced upside down in a field, crushing the roof towards me. Then it flew up in the air again and landed right side up, a mangled wreck of metal and earth.

All was uncannily still. I sat for a few moments, stunned, before I tried the door handle. To my surprise, it opened first time. I fell out, and – on unsteady legs – ran the mile or so to the nearest village, where my in-laws lived. I pounded at their door and shouted through the letter-box.

That morning I did not read the news. I *was* the news. *CNFM News at 7.00. A CNFM reporter narrowly escaped death when his car skidded off a wet country lane in the early hours of this morning.*

I still have flashbacks to that moment. I still clearly recall the numbing terror as the car careered to and fro on the wet road, how it felt to fly out of control, not knowing where I might land – even whether I would be alive when I did. Such an experience leaves you profoundly shaken, even years later. Having stared death close in the face, you can never again look at life through the same eyes.

THE GIFT OF BEING

No longer could I take life for granted. Simply being had seemed the most inconsequential of feats, a dull precondition for the excitement of doing. Now the brute fact of existence was itself a miracle. An unexpected gift. That day in 1990 when I wrote off the car, and almost wrote myself out of the script of this life, something in my attitude towards the everyday shifted, fundamentally and irreversibly. I became struck by the obvious fact that everything which is there – a stone, a tree, a house, a discarded piece of chewing gum – might not have been. Its existence is not a given. It is a gift.

The most commonplace began to appear new and strange. Faced with the trivial and banal I began to sense that surprise, curiosity, and awe which together produce wonder. In an odd way, the sheer fact that something was there as opposed to not there became striking. I was experiencing the world as a wonderful place.

The word 'is' should make young girls marvel, bank clerks and window-cleaners skip, pensioners throw their hats into the air. Because it is the opposite of 'isn't'. By some gratuitous miracle, the wide, grey domains of 'isn't' have been invaded by the joyful presence of a wild, cheery 'is'. With every 'is', the realms of non-being have been once again ravaged by something alien. Something has hovered over waste and void, and has spoken existence into being. And the least we can do each morning is to shout a heartfelt 'Thanks!'

Like Damocles' sword of ancient legend, life itself hangs by a slender thread. It is only when the sword falls or threatens to fall that you grow to appreciate the delicacy, strength and beauty of the thread which has held it.

It is one of the paradoxes of life that we most fully appreciate something when its absence looms or becomes a reality. That which was banal leaves a gaping hole when it is gone. The book, CD or piece of gardening equipment might stand untouched for years. But we give it away and it instantly becomes the very thing necessary for survival. Our usual radio channel becomes infinitely desirable when we are travelling outside our own country. 'My mother had one, but she gave it away' is the dismal call of the penitent complacent.

The art of wonder is the lost art of astonishment. Wonder is an attitude to life and creation which takes nothing for granted, which knows that each molecule just might not have been there, given different circumstances. Wonder is the treasuring of the miraculous in the mundane. It is the refusal to take for granted even the most prosaic aspects of the daily round. It is a rediscovery of a bright twinkle on the items whose sheen has been dulled by familiarity.

Wonder is the rediscovery of people. Under its benevolent sway we are urged to focus not so much on the routine irritation of mislaid slippers, as on the alarming piece of experimental art that is the human foot. Wonder is encountering those around us with open-mouthed surprise, as if they were the most eccentric strangers we had ever met. It is telling those closest to us all the sentimental, adoring things we will one day put in their funeral oration. But the trick with wonder is to do it while they are still alive.

Wonder is gratitude for the fat, chuckling 'is' which constitutes our earthly existence, an amazement which takes nothing for granted.

QUEEN VICTORIA'S GENERATION X

In 1892 an 18-year-old student named Gilbert Keith Chesterton began his studies at the Slade School of Art in London. His time at the Slade coincided with a period of intense inner turmoil, a state aggravated by the spirit of the age in which he was living. Some people imagine the whole of the Victorian era to have been a time of stern religious absolutes and prim moralizing. Far from it. By the 1890s, Chesterton's generation was swimming in a tide of *fin-de-siècle* decadence and intellectual cynicism, an atmosphere which profoundly influenced the young art student.

The bohemian Chesterton, like so many of his contemporaries, took pot shots at religious dogma of any kind, and reserved particular scorn for the clergy, whom he saw as playing at little more than power games. Alongside his religious cynicism went an attitude of scepticism towards life and the outside world: that adolescent sense that he alone was the centre of the universe, and that without his own mind, it might all prove to be an illusion. Did the natural world exist, outside his own imagining? Did other people have any objective existence, aside from his perceptions of them? It was an attitude of philosophical scepticism which would anticipate much of the thinking of the late 20th century.

His creed of the time was a kind of romantic humanism. No need for God; humanity would manage to forge its own way to a glorious future. Humankind alone is divine, and all the superstitions, dogmas and myths of the ages are no more than projections of our own desires onto the canvas of the universe.

However, as he was to note in later life, once a man stops believing in God, he does not believe in nothing – he believes in anything. And Chesterton was also fascinated by the macabre and occult. His notebooks from the time are haunted by drawings of goblins and devils, their crooked grins betraying his obsession with evil. His rejection of an earlier Victorian religiosity led to a dabbling with spiritualism and the Ouija board. He also appears to have been drawn, perhaps unconsciously, to the more lurid and masochistic side of sexuality. His earlier school notebooks show doodles of people with hands tied behind their backs, and naked figures being whipped. His imagination ran riot.

The mindset of this art student at the close of the 19th century sounds curiously familiar 100 years later: a dying century; dissatisfaction with the fading dreams of an earlier generation; mistrust of institutional religion; truth claims seen as little more than power games; fascination with decadence; romantic glorification of suicide; dabbling in a potpourri of occult and oriental mysticisms (the late 19th century saw the first big turn to the East in the search for spiritual enlightenment); fascination with the violent side of sexuality; loneliness; the rise of drug-taking; a relishing of anything which promises to titillate a jaded palate. And yet it was an age profoundly searching for meaning, hope and intimacy: a longing for truth, for relationships, for God.

We have been here before. Chesterton and his turbulent days as a student closely parallels the late 20th century's own Generation X, product of our own turmoil, as we shall explore.

LIGHT IN THE TUNNEL

By the end of his time at the Slade in 1895, a profound shift was beginning to occur in Chesterton. So much so that in later life he looked back on his student days as a time of darkness, even madness. In his *Autobiography*, he records how he had felt himself 'plunging deeper and deeper as in a blind spiritual suicide'.[1]

What brought about the change? It appears to have been a combination of factors. Firstly, the experience of close, intimate relationships with other people. A fascination with evil is often sparked by the loneliness of adolescence. So it was with Chesterton. As he entered his twenties he renewed old boyhood friendships, including his acquaintance with the writer E.C. Bentley, and through this friendship seems to have come a clearer vision of goodness and the virtues of trust and loyalty. The experience of openness to another human being tugged Chesterton beyond the morbid confines of his own mind, a liberation for which he was profoundly grateful.

At the same time, he increasingly realized that the forbidden lure of the black arts was failing to come up with the goods. In his *Autobiography* he recalls how sessions with the Ouija board at that time would leave him not with secret powers and spiritual insight, but with an aching head and a bad taste in the mouth, or – as he put it – 'a bad smell in the mind'.[2] Disillusioned and sickened by the occult, he was becoming more and more open to a new, positive vision of the world around him.

One place he found this was in the writings of the American poet Walt Whitman. In Whitman he encountered a zest for life, a slap in the face of decadence and pessimism, and a sense of the dignity and nobility of humankind. Gradually he became more cynical towards the fashionable cynicism of his day. He began to doubt his own doubting, and grew bored with boredom.

All this time Chesterton had not yet begun seriously to reconsider the orthodox Christianity dumped by his contemporaries. That was to begin the following year when he met his wife-to-be, Frances, a practising Christian. For now, all he knew was that he had become sceptical of scepticism, indifferent to moral indifference, and was becoming an increasingly intrigued reader of the Bible. By the age of 21, as he went to work in the world of publishing, he found himself newly fascinated by the wonder of the humdrum. He was rediscovering a sense of astonishment at the mundane and was bursting with gratitude for the sheer gift of life. Before long, the missing piece of the puzzle would be put into place. He would find that the gratitude welling up inside was the natural, instinctive response of the recipient to the giver, the response of a creature towards the Creator.

He was awaking to wonder. The great, good-humoured sanity, which was to characterize his life and work, was stirred through a renewal of wonder in relationships with other people, a renewal of wonder at the earth, and the first inklings of a wonder towards God.

HOME IS A STRANGE LAND

Towards the end of his time at the Slade, as he was beginning to cast off his fashionable morbidity and scepticism, Chesterton wrote a short story entitled 'Homesick at Home'.[3] It tells the story of a man called White Wynd who had been born, raised, married and had raised a family in the same white farmhouse by a river. One day the man becomes angry, restless and – paradoxically – stricken with homesickness. He longs for home, even though he has never once left his own farmhouse.

Despite the entreaties of his family, he sets out around the world to discover the excitement of new horizons. After countless adventures, he reaches the very end of the world. And it dawns on him that the place he has reached is the white farmhouse by the river, his own wife, his own children. And it is the most beautiful place he has ever seen. He has returned home and seen the familiar with new eyes, and it will never be the same again.

The story charts Chesterton's own realization of how sheer habit can dull our astonishment at that which is ours. The most miraculous place we will ever go to is home, and to see it as for the first time. But to realize this, most of us need to lose it for a while, or at least lose our grip on it. His parable suggests the shortest way home might be to go round the world, and see the familiar through new eyes. 'Homesick at Home' is Chesterton's own story, the drama of someone escaping from lethargy and decadence to rediscover the wonder of the commonplace. It was this sense of wonder at the everyday which would run like a silver thread through Chesterton's massive literary output of poems, plays, novels and journalism, until his death in 1936.

In a collection of essays from 1905, *Heretics*, Chesterton offers an example of how we can become desensitized to wonder by overfamiliarity. He tells how a sub-editor at a publishing company where he was working entered the room, cynically wielding a book with some such title as 'Mr Smith' or 'The Smith Family', and observing that a book with such a title could harbour nothing of the mysterious or romantic about it. Chesterton, in reply, points out that, on the contrary,

> In the case of Smith, the name is so poetical that it must be an arduous and heroic matter for the man to live up to it. The brute repose of Nature, the passionate cunning of man, the strongest of earthly metals, the weirdest of earthly

elements, the unconquerable iron subdued by its only con-
queror, the wheel and ploughshare, the sword and steam
hammer, the arraying of armies and the whole legend of
arms, all these things are written, briefly indeed, but quite
legibly, on the visiting-card of Mr Smith.[4]

He reminds us that any perceived dullness lies not in the name
of Smith, 'this name made of iron and flame', but in the dullness
of our own minds, the dullness of eyes that can no longer see
the sparks and the clash of metal.

Perhaps Chesterton's greatest and most enduring work is
his rousing 1908 defence of Christianity against its cultured
despisers, *Orthodoxy*. In the second paragraph of the book, he
writes that he has long fancied writing a novel about a yachtsman who miscalculated his course and 'discovered' England
under the impression that it was some new island in the South
Seas. He says that he himself is that yachtsman. He had allowed
his imagination to set sail into wild, fantastic regions, deep
with mystery and colour. He set out to encounter the new and
exotic, only to find that he arrived at the shores of historic
Christianity, and discover that it was indeed a strange country.
In *Orthodoxy*, Chesterton applies the experience of White Wynd
to the whole human race, a people whose familiarity with
revealed religion has obscured its restless passion and beauty.
We will not appreciate the beauty and scandal of historic
Christianity, he claims, until a jaded culture learns to see it as
for the first time.

The plump English journalist who set sail for exotic, uncharted regions, only to discover that home itself is a strange
land, is the poet laureate of wonder. Chesterton, escapee from
Queen Victoria's blank generation, is the kind of prophet desperately needed by a new generation for whom life has lost its
sparkle, a culture which has lost its appetite. He is the kind of
doctor desperately needed by a generation which wakes up,
only to discover that its sense of wonder has been surgically
removed.

ABOUT THIS BOOK

The rest of this book charts a conviction that there has been an unparalleled loss of wonder amongst today's young adults, the generation widely known as Baby Busters, or Generation X. Chapters 2 to 6, the bulk of the book, profile and attempt to account for this generation's loss of wonder in three key areas: in relationships, attitudes to the world around us, and towards God.

It was, significantly, the reawakening of wonder in precisely these areas which shook Chesterton from his *fin-de-siècle* daze. And the claim of this book is that it is the promise of a reawakened sense of wonder in these same three areas which holds out a vision of hope to a generation so different from Chesterton's – and yet so alike – some 100 years later.

First, however, comes Chapter 1, in which we ask just what it is about the capacity for wonder towards relationships, the world and God that seems to be so crucial for our sanity and fulfilment. It is, above all, a question of human identity, of the stories we tell about ourselves.

CHAPTER ONE

TELLING STORIES: THE ROOTS OF WONDER

What is *you*, Scout? What is the *you* of *you*? What is the link? Where do *you* begin and end? This *you* thing – is it an invisible silk woven from your memories? Is it a spirit? Is it electric? What exactly *is* it?

Douglas Coupland, Life After God

SPIDERS AT BEDTIME

Tonight I shall sit at my children's bedside and tell them a story. It will be a story about Jeremy, a schoolboy of indeterminate age who lives in suburban West London. His seemingly endless capacity for boredom leads him unwittingly into a range of extraordinary and spine-chilling scrapes which force the listening children under the bedclothes in horror, before the reassuring, heart-warming conclusion involving food and sleep.

TELLING STORIES

A story can also be a way of arranging the odds and ends of life into a single narrative, the story of our own lives. It is the 'big picture' which makes sense of all the daily details, and helps us find our place in a wider scheme of things. It helps us answer questions such as: What is the plot of which my life is a part? What is this character that I am playing? How does it relate to the other characters in the plot? Often we carry our stories unspoken, especially if we move in circles where people do not routinely discuss purpose and meaning.

To call this 'big picture' a story in no way prejudges whether it is true or false. 'Story' here does not mean 'fairy story' or 'fantasy'. Rather, it is used in the sense of an account of history and life, as in 'Story of the Blues', 'Our reporter Jenny Brown has the full story . . .', or the hymn, 'Tell me the old, old story'. It is a description which claims to give true information about the world as it really is.

Most of this book will be taking a closer look at the story, or 'world view', of Generation X, the dominant lifestory being told by young adults in the West at the close of one millennium and the start of another. Our aim will be specifically to contrast this story with that of historic Christianity. But there are other examples of stories which offer a plot for understanding life and our role in it. One such is the story told by Siddharta Gautama, otherwise known as Buddha.

For many of today's cultural leaders – media personalities, rock musicians, fashion industry professionals – the spiritual path which feels comfortable is the way of the Buddha. We live in a culture where the lifestyles of the rich and stylish are widely emulated, and there has correspondingly been a widespread revival of interest in Buddhism amongst image-conscious Westerners in search of spiritual truth.

THE ILLUSION OF SELF – BUDDHA'S STORY

For the Buddhist, the story of the universe progresses by moving round and round in circles. This circular plot is best summed up in the so-called 'Four Noble Truths' discovered by the Indian prince, Siddharta Gautama, as he sat in contemplation under a fig tree in the 5th century BC. For Gautama (or Buddha – the enlightened one – as he became known), the first truth is that all of life is suffering. In fact, existence and suffering are one and the same thing. This suffering is due to the accumulation of *karma*, a kind of law of cause and effect. We reap the negative results of actions in a previous existence.

According to the second truth, our suffering is caused because we are too attached to the material world. In particular, it results from the desires of our senses. The third truth claims that it is possible for suffering to cease. Here lies the heart of the Buddhist story: achieving freedom from the cycle of rebirth and suffering. For the Buddha and his followers, to attain 'enlightenment' is to transcend, or rise above, the cycles of reincarnation and suffering. The fourth truth says this can be achieved through following the Eightfold Path, Gautama's teaching on lifestyle.

This Path includes exercises to correct wrong understandings and other unhelpful aspects of lifestyle. It also includes a range of mental disciplines. The goal of it all is *nirvana*, a kind of absorption into an impersonal absolute, an escape from the cycle of rebirths and the determining effects of *karma*. Through meditation, the Buddhist believes she can experience *nirvana* before death, so meditation becomes a crucial part of the Buddhist life.

Unlike some stories, such as that told by Christians, the character of God is absent from the Buddhist tale. Some popular forms of Buddhism involve prayer and a range of spirits and deities. But the teaching of Gautama, as preserved in the purest forms of Buddhism, was agnostic on the question of God. God was irrelevant in the quest for enlightenment. Gautama Buddha never said he was a god, or even a prophet. He was a man who claimed to have found a unique teaching or special knowledge which gave insight into the story of the universe and our place in it. But even more striking than Buddhism's denial of God is its denial of the human self.

According to Gautama, one of the illusions of life which we need to ditch is the belief that 'I' exist at all. It may appear to us that we are separate, independent beings, but this is all an illusion. Our sense that there is 'something else' out there – another person, a mountain, a dog or a tree – is all

13

wrong. I might think of myself as 'myself', but this is due to a kind of cosmic confusion. In meditation, I aim to rid myself of the illusion that I own a unique, individual personality. The 20th-century Tibetan Buddhist master Chögyam Trungpa expresses this illusion of 'self' in the following terms:

> It is as if one of the grains of sand had stuck its neck out and begun to look around. We are that grain of sand, coming to the conclusion of our separateness. This is the 'birth of ignorance' in its first stage, a kind of chemical reaction. Duality has begun.[1]

For the Buddhist there is not even a single 'self' or 'soul' which remains constant through the cycle of rebirths. The only constant is the inherited *karma*.

So the story told by a Buddhist enables him to find his place in the world. His story tells him that while he may see himself as a unique individual, this is a mistake. Life is a cycle of reincarnations, of which his present existence is just one, and he has inherited *karma* from an earlier 'rebirth'. His goal is to escape from the circle into *nirvana*. Then he will leave behind his present experiences of suffering, his *karma*, and the illusion of self. For the time being, his absorption into *nirvana* can be anticipated through meditation.

As for life in the physical world and relationships with other people: at best they offer a training ground in learning detachment from natural human desires. At worst, all such externals as people and things are worthless, illusions derived from the basic error that I and they are separate from each other.

THE ROAD AND THE MILESTONES – THE CHRISTIAN STORY

The Christian story offers a very different account of plot and characterization.

The Christian storyline moves not in circles, but straight ahead. The history of our world is a long road, punctuated by a number of milestones which are God's acts of self-revelation. Each of these milestones divides up the road into different eras of history, which can be plotted in a diagram, as follows:

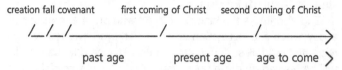

For the Christian this time-line, traced in the Bible from Genesis to Revelation, is the key to understanding the plot of history and our place in it. God creates a world teeming with abundant life, and declares it 'very good'. One part of that creation is humanity who, not content with being dependent creatures, offers a unilateral declaration of independence to the Creator. Because people were never designed to be independent from God's provision, the result is a 'fall' from the perfection they had previously enjoyed.

The human world is now marred by sin: a state of rebellion, or 'missing the mark', which has a ripple effect into the rest of creation. God now has a choice. He can either abandon the broken earth or else bring a rescue plan into effect. Because his very nature is total love and self-giving, he chooses rescue.

The first stage of the rescue plan is known as the covenant with Israel. God chooses one old man from a city near the Persian Gulf, and makes a promise to him. The promise is that his extended family will be a prototype of what humanity could look like when restored to intimacy with God. They are to model this restored relationship to the rest of creation, so that in time the whole world will be drawn in. The old man's name is Abram (soon to be changed to Abraham), his descendants the people of Israel.

Since the effects of sin are still pervasive, part one of God's rescue plan includes provisions for dealing with its effects. Because sin poisons society and relationships between people, God gives the young nation a range of laws to enable them to live together in relative peace. And because sin poisons the relationship between people and God, he gives them a means for dealing with the blockage. Blood shed in sacrifices gains freedom from sin for the person offering it up. There is a sub-stitution – animal for person.

God also litters the history of Israel with prophetic visions of a day when the perfection so briefly enjoyed in Eden will be recreated, and all suffering and sin erased. One day there really will be heaven on earth once again. And here is a crucial point: the biblical vision of eternity is not the immortality of a soul, drifting around like an unpegged nightshirt in an ethereal heaven. The vision is a renewed, physical earth populated by renewed, physical human beings and animals. It is to be a state of what the people of Israel call *shalom*: unhindered intimacy between people, the earth and God.

Then, in the first century AD, comes the most decisive mile-stone of all. God himself walks the earth as a human being. Jesus of Nazareth announces and demonstrates that the eagerly awaited age to come has started to break into the present age – in his own person. The health of the future age breaks in in the miracles of healing; the salvation of the future age breaks in through acts of forgiveness; the justice of the future age breaks in as Jesus offers dignity to those denied it; a quality of personal relationships from the future age breaks in as Jesus gathers around him a motley collection of the society of his day. Jesus, God in human flesh and prototype citizen of God's future age, begins to bring the reality of the future into the present.

Ultimately, Jesus is killed. To passers-by it looks like any other criminal execution by the Roman authorities. But from the perspective of God's story, the death of Jesus is a final sacrifice for sin. No longer is sin a barrier between people and God. Jesus's bodily resurrection is both God's vindication of the life and death of Jesus, and also a foretaste that we too can one day experience resurrection from death. Finally, the story cul-minates in the return of Jesus to earth, to bring in the promised age in all its fullness. And that great climax of history is still future.

It is only within this plot that a Christian can make sense of her place in God's story. She will locate herself somewhere around the middle of the time-line of history: able to look back to the 'past age', or first part of God's rescue plan, and forward to its culmination in the 'age to come'. Whether she is still at the start of the 'present age' of history, or near its close, only time will tell.

She knows she is living in a time of tension, the 'already but not yet' chapters of the plot, and this accounts for the mixed messages she encounters daily in life and faith. She knows the reality of sin obliterated; she has started to experience the reality of the age to come in her relationships with people, the world about her, and with God; but the future fullness of God's reign on the earth has not yet come. She still suffers, questions and doubts. She still fails to live out the love she so acutely craves and longs to show others.

This is a rapid overview of the plot of the Christian story. What of characterization? Unlike the story of Gautama, it affirms with vigour the centrality of God. Far from a cosmic absence or impersonal force, God is real and personal – the source of all personality. When Moses asks God who he is, the answer is stark and simple. He is who he is: 'God said to Moses, "I am who I am. This is what you are to say to the Israelites: 'I AM has sent me to you'"' (Exodus 3.14).

Similarly, individual human personality is not an illusion; it is real. We are created as truly separate 'selves', made to relate to others and the world around us. All of this is encapsulated in the words used by the author of Genesis to describe human nature. We are the 'image of God'.

THE IMAGE

The phrase is from the very first chapter of the Bible. The poet has already evoked the origins of the earth, the skies, the oceans, plant life and animal life, and now his tumbling torrent of Hebraic verse reaches a crescendo:

17

Then God said, 'Let us make man in our image, in our like-ness, and let them rule over the fish of the sea and the birds of the air, over the livestock, over all the earth, and over all the creatures that move along the ground.'

So God created man
in his own image,
in the image of God
he created him;
male and female
he created them. (Genesis 1.26, 27)

It is this insight into identity which gives the Christian a key to understanding her own character in the universal story.

First we need to grasp the background to the idea of 'image' in the ancient world. It was a common practice of rulers in the Ancient Near East to leave images or statues of themselves in the provinces of their empire. These images would represent the might and majesty of the ruler to those who could not see him in person. In the same way, the coins of the Ancient Near East – like our own – carried the stamped image of the monarch, another standing reminder of who was boss.

Humanity is on the earth as a visible reminder of the majesty of the invisible God. We are his representatives on earth, reminding the rest of creation of the reality of its Creator. The 'image' of God is not just some dimension of our make-up, such as a capacity for reason, speech or feeling. Instead, simply by being human we are God's imagers on earth. 'God' is written all the way through us, like the lettering in sticks of peppermint rock from English seaside resorts.

This has profound implications for who I am as a person, as well as how I live my life, in three crucial areas: my relations with other people, my relations with the world about me, and my spiritual journey.

IMAGE AS RELATIONSHIP

The image of God does not only apply to me as an individual.

It is something which binds me to other people. On the face of it, it seems strange that God should speak in plurals. Why not say: 'Let me make man in my image'? One possibility is that God is referring to his heavenly court, all the other spiritual beings who worship in his presence. Perhaps he is shouting in excitement to all the heavenly host: 'Look over here! You'll never guess what I've just made!' The book of Job reminds us that at the creation, 'all the angels shouted for joy' (Job 38.7). However, a fuller insight into the community of heaven comes with the New Testament revelation of God as trinity, one God in three persons. Not only is he Father, but also Son (Jesus), and Holy Spirit (the empowering presence of God who indwells believers). The God who has always been a trinity is revealed on earth as trinity with the incarnation of the Son and the sending of the Spirit.

I am, then, the image on earth of a God who is three persons, who is relationship and intimacy in his own being. Love is not a tacked-on, optional extra. It is intrinsic to who God is and, by extension, who I am. I relate, therefore I am.

IMAGE AS STEWARDSHIP

However, being the image of God is more than being relational. It also helps define the way people relate to the earth. Being human means embodying the nature of God, and the truth of who is really in charge on earth, for the benefit of the rest of creation. We are God's managers of the earth.

We have a calling, individually and in community, to tend the earth and draw out its potential. Not just for our own sakes, although this is important, but for God's sake. One dimension of this calling is ecological, the calling to protect and care for the earth by careful use of resources. No good manager stands by twiddling his thumbs while the object of his care is being destroyed.

But there is more to our calling on earth than fire-fighting. In the verse immediately following the creation of humanity in God's image, we are told: 'God blessed them and said to them,

"Be fruitful and increase in number; fill the earth and subdue it. Rule over the fish of the sea and the birds of the air and over every living creature that moves on the ground"' (Genesis 1.28). This verse is sometimes called the 'cultural mandate' to humans. They are to take the raw materials of the earth and use them creatively. They are not simply to live 'close to nature' (as many Romantics and ecologists would have it), but to be creative and cultural. God in effect tells his newly created image that he has left their earth unfinished. It is now over to them to draw out its latent potential in terms of agriculture, the arts, economics, architecture, science, and so on. It is as we carry out our distinctive callings to be teachers, fashion designers, politicians, road-sweepers, musicians, students, business executives and artists that we live as the image of God on earth. We are called to be creative stewards of creation.

IMAGE AS WORSHIP

There is, however, something even more primary than our call to relationship and stewardship. And that is our relationship to God himself. This is because at the core of my very being I have a special standing before God. I am created out of love by a God who is love, and called to love him. Our dignity and destiny can be found only in relation to God. We find purpose and identity only as we relate to him.

The way this is to be lived out at the close of the second millennium AD is summed up in the title of the old hymn: 'Trust and obey'. We trust God to hold us, guide us and inspire us. As we do so, we throw down a gauntlet to all other philosophies and '-isms' which claim to find meaning and purpose elsewhere. We are also called to obey, not a popular concept in a culture which tells us that we only find fulfilment in freedom, independence, finding the truth our own way.

Here is a paradox: that limits can be freeing. Our culture trains us to define liberation as freedom from all restraint. But autonomy is not liberating for people created for relationship, any more than it is liberating to 'free' a creature from its natural element. We do a goldfish no favours if we pull it from its bowl, take it to see a movie and force it to eat popcorn.

So the Christian believes in developing a lifestyle obedient and pleasing to God. This does not restrict her freedom, but brings freedom. We can put this in terms of stories again. A character created to live in one story is unlikely to thrive in another, alien, story. If the ugly duckling remains in the plot-line of Hans Christian Andersen's fairy story, he discovers his true identity as a swan. But make him trip-trip-trap over a bridge ruled by an ogre and he'll soon find he's duckling *à l'orange*.

Liberty, freedom and autonomy are meaningless without reference to a bigger story. In the Christian story the paradox is that we only discover liberation when we acknowledge our call to obedience.

Here, for the Christian, lies something of the importance of Jesus of Nazareth. Not only is he Son of God, dying to negate sin and rising to bring new life. He also embodies in his earthly life all that humanity was created to be: in relationship to God and in obedience to God. He is the one who fully images God on earth, the new Adam, prototype of the new humanity. Our goal is to be transformed ever more into his image: 'And we, who with unveiled faces all reflect the Lord's glory, are being transformed into his likeness with ever-increasing glory, which comes from the Lord, who is the Spirit' (2 Corinthians 3.18). Needless to say, to be transformed into the image of Christ is not to become a first-century Jewish male woodworker. It is that I discover what I am uniquely capable of becoming as my own story builds to its climax. I can only discover the true 'me' in relation to God.

TURNING INWARDS, TURNING OUTWARDS

In the last chapter we looked at the young G.K. Chesterton, living in the late 19th century. Here is another true story, about somebody at the end of the 20th century. Dan, a student, is preoccupied with questions of identity. Who am I? What is the real me? Why do I seem to be so different at home, with my friends, at college? Is there any solid 'core' that is me at all? How do I find fulfilment in life?

He has been born into a culture which, for at least the past 200 years, has told him that the answer to these questions lies in a stable, unchanging 'self' that is his own and which he simply needs to 'discover'. He is an individual, whose academic and social education has trained him to stand on his own two feet, to be independent. The few bits of religious writing he has read also tell him to look for the answers within, digging into his own psyche.

So he digs and he digs. But he cannot find a great deal. What is the point of looking for the answers within if there is nothing much there? So he sits in his college room, listening to his CD collection, going deeper and deeper into his own mind, and begins increasingly to use nicotine and alcohol in an attempt to stimulate a jaded palate.

It is only when Dan eventually begins to get out of his own room and join some new clubs and societies that things start to change. The paradox of Dan's situation is that it is only when he is wrenched out of his own armchair and abandons the excavations into his own brain, that he starts to find himself. He can only come alive when he finds himself in relationship with that which is other than himself.

We can illustrate the point diagrammatically. For several hundred years the West has worked on a 'snooker ball' model of identity, which sees the self as a hard, enclosed unit which will sometimes bounce off other balls: friends, neighbours, God, and so on. Each of these balls rolls around on the green surface of the snooker table, until each is finally potted into a hole and leaves the game (see illustration).

Every ball, on this model, is fundamentally separate, but will occasionally touch other balls, even have its own course changed by them. The self, however, remains impregnable.

On the other hand, the biblical model is inescapably relational. The three key relationships in which I participate are not

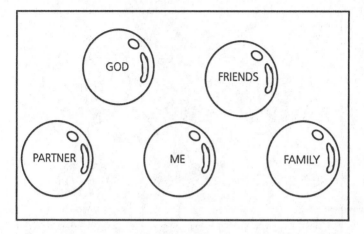

simply other balls, knocking me in a particular direction. A wholly different picture is needed to convey what it is to be in the image of God, a more organic image such as that of a tree in a forest.

For a tree, non-dependent, non-relational existence is an impossibility. It must relate to the earth below for its water and nutrients, to the sky above for sunlight and oxygen. It is also in relationship with the other vegetation around it. Each of the relationships is in some sense dynamic and mutual. Just so, we too interact with, and are substantially defined by, our relationships: with other people, with the world and with God (see overleaf).

The claim that we only exist in relationship should come as no surprise to anybody who takes the Christian story seriously. The Christian account of characterization denies that the personality is an illusion ('the true self does not exist'), and that it is self-sufficient ('find the answers within'). Rather, every character is unique. Each is created by a loving Creator and has worth in his eyes. The self is stable, but not fixed or static; the only truly static people are corpses.

In fact, if we take seriously the Christian vision of living one day on a renewed earth, we will discover our 'true' selves not so

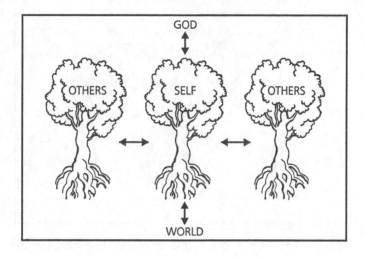

much by delving into our present psyche, as by being oriented towards the future – what we are capable of becoming. The search for true identity urges us to journey, like Bunyan's pilgrim, ever onwards into the future: 'What we will be has not yet been made known. But we know that when he appears, we shall be like him, for we shall see him as he is' (1 John 3.2). To be human is to be on the move.

Somebody might ask: if everybody has to find their identity from the same three sources, what makes us different from each other? The answer is that the author might have put us in the same story, but he has assigned each of us a different character or role. As I look to God, I am unique because he knows me by name. It is engraved on the palm of his hand, a standing reminder that he thinks I am wonderful (see Isaiah 49.16).

As I relate to the world I am unique because nobody else inhabits the same patch of earth as me at this point in the story. Nobody else has travelled exactly the same path as me, or has the same stewardship-calling (vocation) as me. And I am unique as I relate to other people, because nobody else has the same network of relationships as I do. The three basic principles of identity are stable. But the details are unique and particular to each one of us.

MADE FOR WONDER

Little surprise, then, that it was the rediscovery of these three things – relationship, stewardship and worship – which awoke Chesterton to wonder. Together they lead us into an encounter with something, or somebody, different from ourselves. They each open us up and make us vulnerable to that which is 'other'. Relationship opens us up to an encounter with other people; stewardship opens us up to an encounter with our physical environment; worship opens us up to an encounter with God. To be open to the otherness found in relationship, stewardship and worship is to inhabit a world where reality constantly jumps out at us from behind a bush and surprises us.

To be human, according to the Christian story, is to root our identity in a dynamic interplay with other people, the earth and God. It is also to find joy and astonishment in these same areas. It is to be open to wonder.

It also follows that if the wellsprings of wonder dry up, our identities will grow parched and wonder will evaporate. And here is precisely our dilemma at the close of the second millennium.

CHAPTER TWO

GENERATION X:
A LOSS OF WONDER

She says she remembers another thing about when she was young – she remembers when the world was full of wonder – when life was a strand of magic moments strung together, a succession of mysteries revealed . . . She doesn't know how to reclaim that sense of magic any more . . .

Douglas Coupland, *Life After God*

BOOM OR BUST?

Today's generation of young adults has been called many things, not all of them polite. Terms which have stuck include Baby Busters, the Lost Generation, the Blank Generation and, increasingly, Generation X – a term popularized by the Canadian writer Douglas Coupland in his 1992 novel of that title.

The ugly term Baby Busters defines them by comparison with an earlier generation, the Baby Boomers – those born between the end of the Second World War and the 1960s. Fuelled by the dreams of comfort and unprecedented prosperity, the birth rate to couples in the West soared during this period, leading to a 'boom' in births. However, from the 1960s to the 1980s, the numbers tailed off drastically, or went 'bust', due in part to the explosion in contraception and abortion in the 1960s. In the United States, one in three pregnancies was aborted during the 1970s and '80s. It is the unaborted of that generation who have now reached adulthood.

To identify an Xer more precisely is not as simple as it might appear. In the USA and Canada many sociologists define them as those born between 1961 and 1981. However, this apparently simple dating is complicated by two factors. Firstly, no cultural change happens overnight. There will always be those born in the transitional period, at the tail end of one generation, at the start of the other, and belonging fully to neither. Secondly, with many shifts in social and cultural trends, there is often a time-lag between North America and the rest of the English-speaking world. This is likely to push back the dating of Europe's Generation X some years later than their counterparts in the States.

Can we, then, identify who counts as Generation X? The earliest possible birth date we could ascribe to those who were to become Xers is 1961. It might be more accurate to describe those born during the first half of the '60s as 'Overlappers' or 'Tweeners': not quite Boomers, not yet fully fledged Busters. My own observation of youth in the UK and Europe is that those who became our Generation X had not been born before the late '60s, perhaps as late as 1970 – certainly, a good few years after their American counterparts. Before the '60s, definitely a Boomer, from the '70s definitely a Buster. In between, a hazy area where one fades into the other. On this reckoning, I and my contemporaries – born in the UK in 1963 – would count as Tweeners, but with a bias towards the values of Boomerdom.

Dates give an approximate guide to identifying Generation X. But to be an Xer is less about calendars than a state of mind. Theirs is a distinctive attitude towards life, forged in opposition to what went before, a flat rejection of most that Baby Boomers hold dear. At the risk of oversimplifying, Boomers are 'yuppies', driven by success, career, achievement, prosperity, comfort. They are a 'me first' generation, shaped by Thatcherism and Reaganomics.

Xers, on the other hand, feel excluded from the Boomer

dream. Not only could they never attain such goals, they see them as the wrong goals in the first place. Generation X is not simply a late phase of the baby boom. It is the vanguard of a new, emerging culture which has fundamentally different ideals. Xers are more likely to value relationships above success, community above fixed goals, personal authenticity above achievement. Xers are not so much a 'me' generation as a 'we' generation. Boomers still tend to have a touching faith that science and technology will solve our problems. Busters know they never will, and could even make the problems worse. If Boomers have some residual trust in historic national institutions such as government, political parties, police and religious bodies, Busters have almost none.

But there is another, less tangible, difference between Boomers and Busters. It has something to do with a way of looking at the world. The Boomer mentality encourages people to be pushy, driven, go-getting. In a word, to achieve. Xers looking at such values shrug their shoulders. What's the point?

The term 'blank generation' embodies the popular media stereotype of Busters as bored, lethargic, and without the zest or idealism which ought to characterize youth. All too often Xers are only too happy to fit the stereotype, cultivating a posture of cynical world-weariness and apathy. To their elders, so many Xers appear to be depressed and numbed to life, and this is borne out by the dramatic rise in suicides amongst that generation. In the decade between 1982 and 1992, there was a rise in suicides amongst UK males between the ages of 15 and 24 of a massive 71 per cent. There is a level of depression, anger and a rock-bottom self-esteem felt by Generation X which has no precedent in our culture, and is beginning to alarm those of older generations.

Yet Xers are not without hopes, dreams or visions. They are a generation yearning for a better world and utterly committed to depth and integrity in human relationships. It is a generation more open to questions of meaning and spirituality than any other in the West over the past 200 years, as we shall explore in the final chapter.

To find a very real idealism and spiritual hunger coinciding with such a degree of apparent pessimism, despair and apathy is unprecedented in our culture. To understand how each has now become a different side of the same coin, we first need to understand a little background. A good place to start is with the question of how any of us makes sense of our own identity.

LOSING THE PLOT

We have said that personal identity comes through a capacity to extend the self backwards and forwards in time: I can remember the past and make plans for the future. My sense of self is stable because it has continuity through my own small stretch of history, in the wider context of God's big history. We have also said that identity is forged in relationship. In particular, the three vital relationships with other people, the world around us, and with God. These three relationships also have the by-product of provoking a sense of astonishment and wonder as we are pulled beyond ourselves into a dynamic encounter with 'otherness'.

Now imagine, for a moment, a generation for whom every one of these roots of identity and wonder has been severed. A generation denied any real sense of a meaningful past, or hope for the future. A generation without a big story, either for an individual life or for the world. And imagine a generation incapable of forming authentic relationships with other people, which has a damaged relationship with the earth, and which has lost any meaningful concept of God, let alone a God who can be known and met through personal encounter.

Such a generation would be rootless, aimless, depressed, alone, numbed, indifferent and almost certainly suicidal. It would be a generation desperately craving what it lacked – the basis for identity and wonder. It would, in other words, be a generation craving roots, purpose in life, intimacy in relation-ships, ecological sensitivity and spirituality.

Generation X has been raised to believe that there is no big story to the universe. Xers are the first generation to grow up in a world infused with the spirit of what has become known as postmodernity. Many thinkers are increasingly dividing the history of the West into three big eras: the premodern (up to the 18th century), the modern (from the 18th century to somewhere around the late 1960s or early '70s), and the postmodern (the present era).

The main characteristic of the postmodern era is that all the big ideas – faiths, philosophies and '-isms' – of the previous two have collapsed. The religious institutions which dominated the premodern era are no longer followed without question. The big ideologies of the modern era have come to nothing. Marxism lies in ruins. A naive faith in reason and science to give us all the answers has resulted in environmental pollution, two World Wars and the threat of global holocaust. Postmodernism is about the end of all such big ideas (or 'grand narratives' as they are often called).

Postmodernity is a general climate or mood of our times. Postmodern*ism* is an ideology, which takes this contemporary *Zeitgeist* and turns its vague spirit into a doctrinaire ideology, centred on 'doing your own thing'. Postmodernism claims that every view is relative and there is no such thing as absolute truth. Something might be 'true' for you, but not for me. Any attempt to persuade somebody of your own opinion or to claim that something is objectively true is seen as playing power games. The postmodern person feels free to 'pick'n'mix' their own customized lifestyle from all the beliefs and styles of history.

But postmodernism is not just ideas. It is a general atmos-phere, conveyed particularly through the popularity of television. TV output is a jumble of styles and unconnected images. Politics, ads, news, soaps and charity appeals all tumble over each other in rapid succession. Boundaries between truth and fiction blur. Like the fashion mags, there is no single 'big story' being told – just images. Style is content.

Xers, who have absorbed the assumptions of postmodernism as easily and readily as they breathe air into their lungs, are doubly bereft of a big story. Not only has postmodernism poured scorn on earlier eras' attempts to find a unifying vision (premodernity and modernity), it denies that any single plotline of history is the true one. Xers are puzzled characters in search of a story.

But this is not all. Any last vestiges of a sense that Xers are part of a story bigger than themselves have been killed off by a series of surgical operations to remove from them both a meaningful past and a hopeful future. This is not the fault of Xers. It is the inheritance they have received from their elders.

LOSS OF THE PAST

Generation X is the most rootless generation in history. Down the ages, people have always known that they grow only by absorbing nourishment from roots which go down deep into their individual, family and national past. However, over the past few decades, these roots have been wrenched out one by one, leaving a generation clinging grimly to the hillside of history, a culture easily uprooted and blown away by any passing blast. The roots which now lie exposed and withering include: family, community, vocation, national pride, religious tradition, shared values, and respect for institutions.

Of course, this is not to say that each of these roots was always healthy. Family could be restrictive and oppressive, national pride could become jingoism, time-honoured institutions have often been a mask for corruption, and so on. But what is beyond question is that they bound a person to a shared past, a past which helped give identity and stability.

For most individuals for most of human history the crucial unit was the wider family. Membership of a tribe, clan, or extended household was fundamental to a person's self-understanding.

It was the place where a person found a sense of belonging and a shared memory of people and events. In the West, this unit then shrank to the nuclear family of two parents and two or three children, which in turn is collapsing under the kinds of strain it was never intended to bear alone. Due to high rates of mobility today, almost no Xer has experience of the support and history offered by a strong wider family unit. Granny lives hundreds of miles away.

In the US around four in ten marriages end in divorce, and of every 100 children, 30 are now born to single mothers. Britain saw a six-fold increase in the divorce rate between 1960 and 1995, and a rise in the proportion of babies born outside marriage from 6 per cent in 1960 to 32 per cent in 1995. One in five UK children now live with a lone parent (compared to one in 13 in the early 1970s).

This is not to point an accusing finger at specific divorcees or single parents, coping admirably in difficult circumstances. But one thing remains certain. The overwhelming weight of research leaves no doubt that divorce is a devastating experience for the children affected. And since almost half of today's twenty-somethings are the products of broken marriages, the result is a generation for whom domestic instability and insecurity is no longer the exception, but has become the norm. It is normal to expect that your parents will not remain together, if you even had two to start with, and to experience the hurts and confusion of family separation.

The result has been tragic for the hordes of divorced Baby Boomers themselves. When yet another friend of mine, barely into his thirties, recently announced he would soon be divorced, I shared his sense of devastation. However, the consequences for the Xer children of Boomer divorcees has been far worse. Their experiences of broken homes have led to a wholesale retreat from long-term commitment in relationships. Xers have seen all too clearly the misery of marriage in the lives of their parents. They have seen at first hand marriages which were abusive and then ended in divorce. This has led to a wholly understandable reluctance to trust others. Xers are a cautious generation. To trust too much, to love too much, is to open a doorway to pain. Far safer to remain emotionally numbed.

Of course, this still leaves the more than half from families which have stayed together. But even if this has given them a stable home background (which cannot be assumed), then their contact with friends means that they too know all too intimately the traumas of a broken home. In his book *A Generation Alone*, the US student chaplain William Mahedy uses the scientific concept of the 'critical mass' to illustrate the point. In the past, the experience of emotional deprivation due to a traumatized and dysfunctional life at home and in the streets unquestionably existed. But it was the exception rather than the rule. For the first time, sufficiently large numbers of Generation Xers have experienced some sort of serious trauma at home and in society to have 'set off a chain reaction of pathology within the entire generation'.[1]

Even changing eating habits can be said to have contributed to the decline of the family as a crucial, supportive unit. Today, families are less likely to meet around a meal table than to 'graze' at whatever time suits individuals. And even the idea of the communal TV dinner is disappearing as more people of younger ages have their own TVs. By 1994, half of all UK seven- to ten-year-olds had a TV in their own room. For 11- to 14-year-olds, the figure rises to no less than seven in ten.

As a result, countless Xers have been denied the primary opportunities to learn about security, openness and trust which have historically been provided by the family unit – both nuclear and wider. The result has been a generation in survival mode, distrustful of others, craving love and security, longing to form close relationships but terrified of being hurt again.

This morning I walked with my two children to school. On the way home I passed a young couple in the street who stood screaming at each other until they were almost hoarse. They were audible several streets away, and their language was violent, abusive and obscene. Holding the woman's hand was a small girl who clung to her mother, wide-eyed and terrified. That small girl will survive. But she will only survive by killing off trust and vulnerability, by learning that you have to deaden yourself to the hurts which others will inflict on you. She has learned the lessons of life modelled by her parents. She is part of a generation which has learned to survive by becoming numbed.

Alongside family, most people through history have been rooted deep in a local community, often with many members of that community sharing a vocation such as agriculture, mining or fishing. A community tells its own stories and cherishes its own memories: the day the roof blew off the town hall, the day the lightning struck old Fred's car, the year the snow was so deep the houses were half buried. Today community is being replaced by mobility. For the first time in history, more people in the world now live in cities than on the land. And movement to the city so often means anonymity, a loss of rootedness. There has been a corresponding rise in loneliness and alienation. Many of us have never even spoken to our neighbours.

This loss of community has almost certainly given rise to the appeal of fictional communities, in which characters know and are known and the community is bound to the past by its memories. We crave close community, even if the downside of this can be a lack of privacy, suspicion of outsiders and a narrow parochialism. Since so many of us lack community in real life, we find it in Garrison Keillor's Lake Wobegon, BBC Radio 4's Ambridge, or TV's Ramsey Street. To enter Keillor's fictionalized Minnesota community, living by memories and time-honoured tradition, where people know and are known, is almost unbearably poignant for so many of today's young adults. It is a picture of a world they have never known and will never know.

Communities often support particular professions. Such professions themselves bind a person to a shared past. You become not simply an autonomous individual, but an inheritor of a tradition. You inherit not only a work contract and a style of work clothes, but also a whole archive of stories about the others who have sailed in the same boat, ploughed the same field, dug the same coal-seams. You inherit tales of joys and sorrows, disasters and triumphs.

Today, however, such continuity of employment is the stuff of old movies and sepia-tinted photos. It is a continuity broken by changing work patterns, such as unemployment following the shut-down of traditional industries. Across the North of England, mining towns have lost the industries which spawned them and shipyards stand idle. For others, the loss of continuity is a result of the sheer range of employment possibilities on offer in our society, and the ease of job mobility. Young people who do stand a chance of getting a job look in bewilderment at the sheer range of options available. Catering? Law? Journalism? Accountancy? Engineering? Retail? Close to home or 600 miles away? Or the other side of the globe? Such choice is in one sense wonderfully liberating and exhilarating. In another sense, it can also be paralysing. Either way, it has largely sounded the death knell for local, family-run concerns.

Generation X has also been denied a heritage of national pride. In the USA, every generation from the early settlers until the late 20th century has seen itself in the tradition of the first Puritan pioneers. They saw themselves building a new Jerusalem, a city on a hill which would stand for truth and liberty. The 'American dream' which fired the Baby Boomers was a secularized version of this religious ideal: Americans flying the flag for freedom, prosperity, opportunity. This ideal was to be enforced around the globe by any means possible – opposing left-wing regimes, exporting American fashion and media, and the Coca-colonization of the world by fast food outlets. Even, it has to be admitted to the Church's shame, one motive for Christian missions was to make 'them' – those of alien cultures and habits – more like 'us' in the culturally enlightened West.

The history of America looks very different from the perspective of Xers. Their nation was built on the oppression and extermination of the native Americans, and the cruel, enforced slavery of Africans. The commemoration, in 1992, of 500 years since Christopher Columbus 'discovered' America was a telling moment. For many Americans over the age of 30 – raised with the annual celebration of Columbus Day – it was a moment of pride at the dawning of the greatest civilization the world has ever seen. For many Xers it was a moment of intense shame, a commemoration of theft, genocide and cruelty.

Britain has its own equivalent of the loss of the American dream: the loss of Empire. It is almost impossible for anybody raised in the latter part of the 20th century to enter the mindset of a generation which honestly believed that Britannia ruled the waves and had a mission to civilize and bring peace and progress to less fortunate areas of the world. Even I, at the tail end of the Baby Boom generation, was brought up with old atlases where half the world was shaded to show it had been brought under the civilizing influence of the British Empire. I well remember books with stories of pith-helmeted, heavily moustached Englishmen bringing the untold benefits of Englishness to 'savages'.

Today's British young adults are more likely to squirm with embarrassment at any suggestion that the country which brought the world the Industrial Revolution and invented concentration camps (during the Boer War) has much to feel proud of. Britain is a country which has lost a place in the world and has yet to forge a new role. This post-imperial implosion appears to have permeated through the whole of the culture. We know about the past and we despise it. The future is uncertain and bleak. The present is characterized by a national loss of direction and self-esteem.

Roots deep into the past were also provided for a given community by shared traditions of religion and explicit moral codes. However, in a world where claims to have religious truth or moral absolutes are interpreted as power plays, what place for time-honoured religious and moral traditions? All too often, scepticism about religious claims is shown to have been warranted as church leaders fall in spectacular style – from Jim and

Tammy Bakker to the latest country parson caught with his cassock down. It is a generation which knows all too well the reality of what the novelist Douglas Coupland calls 'life after God'.

A similar fate has befallen the reputations of most of our great national institutions. The British monarchy is increasingly treated as a disreputable, up-market soap opera. A MORI poll for the *Independent on Sunday* in February 1996 found that only a third of Britons felt its royals had a long-term future, whilst 43 per cent felt it did not.

Respect for government is at an all-time low in the cumulative wake of scandals such as Watergate, Irangate, the Arms for Iraq affair, Whitewater . . . the list seems endless. Xers hear politicians' rhetoric about empowerment, law and order, and economic growth. But the reality experienced daily is that divisions between rich and poor are growing wider, crime is rising, party politics crumbling as single-interest group politics proliferates.

There is widespread cynicism about the police and judiciary, not least after a series of overturned court rulings in the cases of the Guildford Four, Birmingham Six and others. The forces of law and order are perceived by many groups in society as racist and bigoted.

No Future

Generation X has not only lost the past, it has also been denied a purposeful future, both at the global and personal levels. The modernist idea that history is a continual 'ascent of man', a journey of progress to better things, no longer carries credibility.

If any single motif dominates the minds of Xers, it is the destruction of the earth due to human folly. With the collapse of the Iron Curtain in Europe, the prospect of nuclear annihilation was replaced by the threat of environmental catastrophe. The desire to protect the earth from a slow, agonizing death due to pollution or asphyxia has become the core morality for a generation which claims to suspect all moralities. Campaigns to preserve natural habitats against encroaching motorway plans and property developers have taken on a religious fervency. Secularized visions of Armageddon haunt the publicity of Green campaign groups, and marketers cash in on our fears. As we wander round shopping arcades we believe that, Superman-like, we are actually saving the planet. We may buy perfumes, body lotions and T-shirts in the belief that our little purchases will tip the balance. For many Xers, the real question is not what I will be *when* I grow older but *if* I grow older.

The future looks dim for Xers not only in a global sense, but also personally. Prospects of employment seem to grow ever bleaker. Many well-trained Xer college graduates leave for a 'McJob': employment with low pay and few prospects. Still more find they have no job at all. Unlike Boomers, few Xers see a career as a ladder to be climbed. They are more likely to expect a series of varied, short-term posts, with little progression or promise of substantial reward.

Economic prospects appear similarly depressing. Busters are the first generation in the West since the 1930s to have a lower standard of living than their parents. In the US, fully 20 per cent of Generation X live below the poverty line. The number of Britons living on less than half average earnings (the European Union definition of poverty) rose from one household in ten in 1979 to one in three in 1992. And according to the UK's Institute for Fiscal Studies, the weekly income of Britain's poorest 10 per cent fell over the same period from £73 to £61. Many in these categories are Xers, often having to live with their parents to make ends meet. Graduates are now starting to leave college with massive debts from their student loans.

In 1994 the youth organization Voluntary Service Overseas surveyed 1,500 15-year-olds in the UK and in the developing world. One question asked was whether the teenagers believed that the world would be a better place by the year 2000. Two-thirds of those in the developing countries agreed that it would. But only one-third of those in the UK agreed. And in June 1995

38

a MORI poll of middle-class British adults, traditionally the group with the highest aspirations for their children, found that well over 50 per cent believed that the world inherited by their children would be a worse place than that which they experienced in their own childhood. When Bishop Lesslie Newbigin, of the Church of South India, returned to the UK in the mid-1970s, he was asked what he thought he would miss most. He said: 'Hope.'

Another reason to question the future has been provided by the rise in the level of visible street violence. US urban gang warfare and street killings are becoming more commonplace as Xers craving a sense of stability and belonging find it in a peer group on the streets. With the rise of the UK drug culture in the 1990s, such killings have become a real fear in cities such as Manchester, Liverpool, London and Birmingham. In the USA, homicide is now second only to road accidents as the major cause of death among young adults – and only slightly ahead of suicide. For every Xer knifed or shot in the street, more suffer the traumas of bereavement, and others read about it in the press and see the blood-stained pavements on the evening news. And all this is even without the ever present shadow of AIDS.

Christine was an intelligent and attractive American in her mid-twenties. She seemed to have it all going for her. But as we sat on the internal flight from Chicago to Denver, and ended up chatting about her personal hopes and fears for the future, even her bright smile could not hide the underlying note of anxiety: 'Hey, it's scary out there.'

THE ETERNAL NOW

Xers find themselves at the watershed of two millennia, denied a big story and losing the plot of both past and present. What, then, remains to reassure a generation that they exist and have a purpose in existing? All that remains is the present. Unlike most cultures through history, Generation X does not inhabit a story. A story needs a beginning, middle and end; it implies continuity. A story also implies a plot, some sort of progression, direction or purpose. But in a culture which has declared ultimate questions of purpose (What is truth? What is goodness? Who is God? Who is *not* God? What is the goal of life?) unanswerable – and hence unimportant – all that remains is the self, adrift in the present moment, a character without a plot.

Generation X inhabits an eternal now. All that is left is me, in the present moment; my own, physical being. Some observers call ours a therapeutic culture: one where there is no higher value than a sense of personal wellbeing and no higher morality than a Sinatra-esque satisfaction that 'I did it my way'.

Xers are drawn particularly to activities which celebrate immediacy and the body – how it looks and how it feels. It is all that remains after everything else has been weeded out and thrown away. Many of the interests of Xers revolve around the self and its appetites in the present moment: dancing, drug-taking, fashion, bodybuilding, TV and video, shopping, computer and arcade games. To be sure, many of these have been the province of youth for decades. Rarely, however, have youth believed this is all there is to life. But now, with the arrival of virtual reality and computer-generated cyberspace, even the idea that my own material body matters very much is open to question.

There has been a full-scale retreat from a meaningful past and a purposeful future into an aimless, perpetual present.

CREATING IDENTITIES

Not only does the loss of a story mean a loss of plot. It also means a loss of characterization. If the historic roots of character lie exposed and shrivelled, and the plot in which you find your own place has been disowned, where then is identity to be found? The answer is that in an eternal present, identity becomes not so much what you have been given as what you piece together for yourself.

Hence the crucial importance of fashion in a postmodern culture, an importance much greater and quite different in kind from its significance in earlier eras. Up till the late 20th century, and the advent of mass production, stylish clothing was primarily an indicator of rank. To wear finery meant you were among the tiny elite of royalty and nobility who could afford fashion. Today, dress is about expressing a chosen persona. In the absence of any fixed or stable 'givens' of identity, you are whatever you choose to be. We buy into 'off-the-peg' identities, creating the person we are by the way we look. I am what I choose to be. I am the way I look.[2]

Xers' main use of the past is as a museum of styles to browse through in assembling a self for the present. 'Retro chic', the recycling and pastiche of old styles from history, can be fun and creative, but is ultimately a superficial use of the past. Rather than listening to our forebears to gain wisdom we plunder their wardrobes to bolster our flagging sense of self.

Similarly, the present nostalgia boom is symptomatic of a loss of hope for the future. We watch reruns of childhood TV programmes, read childhood comics, and hold '70s theme parties. We cling on grimly to trivia from the days when the world still appeared to hold some wonder, as if we crave a little of that lost astonishment. We look back and venerate the heroes who gave our lives meaning, stability and enjoyment all those years ago: Dastardly and Muttley, Mork and Mindy, John Noakes and Shep.

No Wonder

Far from being the cause of their own plight, Xers are inheritors of it from their society and their elders. The Australian social commentator, Richard Eckersley, describes it as the 'cultural abuse' which has been inflicted on today's young people.[3] Another Australian, the youth worker Fuzz Kitto, is more blunt. Today's youth are 'cultural bastards', denied a full inheritance of roots, security and self-esteem.[4]

41

Cultural bastards lack a healthy measure of the three relationships which constitute being the image of God: relationships with people, with the earth, and with the Creator himself. And this lack means their lives will be an impassioned search for each of them, sometimes consciously but more often, unconsciously. The following chapters will deal with the three lost relationships in turn, charting the loss, attempts to remedy this loss, and – finally – some pointers of hope.

To be a cultural bastard is a devastating inheritance. Not only in terms of a crisis of identity, but also a lost sense of wonder. That sense of wonder which makes the difference between facing the universe with boredom and depression, or with astonishment and a twinkle of gratitude in our eye.

CHAPTER THREE

SEX (PART ONE): THE LOST WONDER OF INTIMACY

> There is no better way to dismantle a personality than to isolate it.
>
> The Princess of Wales, BBC TV's *Panorama*, (1995)

THE DEATH OF SEX: SOME SNAPSHOTS

One of the paradoxes of our sex-obsessed culture is that we have achieved something our Puritan and Victorian forebears never even considered a possibility. We have made sex boring.

Our culture deals with sex the way chocolate manufacturers deal with surreptitious eating amongst employees. Far from banning workers from gorging on chocolate bars, companies encourage them to indulge. For about two weeks, the delighted worker eats as much chocolate as he can. Soon, however, he begins to feel nauseous. As the months go by, chocolate changes from being a forbidden temptation to being something banal, a matter of supreme indifference.

For several weeks I worked at a youth club at a small town in the North of England. As I sat with them on the ripped chairs with our cans of Coke, the group of 14- to 18-year-olds joked about who'd been 'shagging' whom recently. Jonny shagged Tracy who'd also been shagging Dave. Kelly had been shagging

Nev, and Kev and Mick had been shagging quite a few people too. Shagging was an alternative to snooker or the cinema. Stopped you getting quite so bored.

One year I attended a Christian conference, held annually at a British holiday centre. I got talking to one of the girls taken on as casual labour for the holiday season, who told me how every week a minibus came to take large numbers of the teenage staff to the 'clap' (gonorrhoea) clinic in town. Working at that holiday centre offered lots of opportunities for casual sexual encounters with people you might never have to meet again. And the medical profession picked up the pieces.

Every year thousands of young adults fly to Mediterranean resorts for under-thirties' holidays whose publicity scarcely disguises the fact that the whole point is sun, sea and sex, with the emphasis on the sex. In my days as a radio journalist, a young colleague told me tales of her own summer vacation with the leading company behind such holidays. One concerned the nightly 'games' in a Spanish resort, which involved throwing your room keys into a pile, and then performing a 'lucky dip' to see whose bed you would share that night. If you ended up with somebody who made you feel physically sick, too bad. Better luck the following night.

Every weekday the advertising-based paper *Loot* hits the news stands of London. Every day hundreds of ads in the 'personal' section are requests couched in a range of creative euphemisms: 'For adult fun and friendship', 'In need of excitement', 'Fun nights in', 'Adventurous male required', 'Broadminded couples only'. Sex is advertised and requested in the same way as a second-hand lawn-mower. These requests for sex outnumber the number of ads in the 'friendship' section at a ratio of several dozen to one, and many are from married couples. Their ads seek out other couples, and various combinations of people, to join them for casual sex.

Behind each personal ad in *Loot* lies a personal tragedy. It is the tragedy of people made for relational intimacy and vulnerability, now reduced to trawling the low-life of the city for an ever more extreme sexual 'fix'. It is the tragedy of people who have persuaded themselves that faithful intimacy with one partner is dull, so they need to keep pushing back the frontiers of weirdness to approach the thrill they once derived from sex. In order to find their fix, such people run enormous risks of disease, violence, blackmail and rape, not to mention many unseen emotional consequences.

I recently watched the head of a leading UK relationships advice group interviewed on TV. She was asked what her advice for young people was in the area of sexual relationships. After a moment's thought, she offered: 'Sex is better if you fancy the person you're sleeping with.'

Most of my contemporaries no longer make love. They shag, bonk and screw – quickly, anonymously, lovelessly. The generation more pitifully searching for intimacy than any other in history has taken the central sacrament of interpersonal intimacy and killed it dead. We have the dubious privilege of living in the culture which is presiding over the death of eroticism.

Ours is a culture crying out for intimacy, but only able to conceive of accessing it through sex. So desperate were we for intimacy that we ripped the veil off sexuality, threw open a myriad of hidden things to public gaze and indulged to excess. But now we find that somebody, somewhere along the line, was not telling us the truth. Somebody we trusted sent us down a blind alley and we found ourselves robbed of the little intimacy we already had.

THE DEATH OF SEX: WHO PULLED THE TRIGGER?

What went wrong in our relationship with sex? At first sight, it might look as if Generation X is to blame for the death of sex, with its casual, 'fast-food' approach to sexuality and its fear of commitment. On closer inspection, however, it becomes clear that Xers are in reality attempting to resuscitate a corpse which was finished off by somebody else. And a number of older figures can be glimpsed, guiltily skulking into the distance. This group includes a number of economists, '60s permissives, modern marketers, even some conservative Christian clerics. And a suspiciously large number of them appear to be Baby Boomers.

Individualism, or 'me-first-ism', is not a new phenomenon. It has been a central pillar of European thought since the 16th century, and by the 18th century it had become the underlying mindset of our culture. The high-water mark of individualism has been in the post-war years, the era of the Baby Boom, reaching its climax in the Thatcherite '80s. The watchword of an entire culture became personal freedom: freedom of choice, freedom to own, freedom to earn and to succeed. The economic theories of Adam Smith (1723–90), which emphasized progress through self-interest, became enshrined at the heart of the burgeoning creed of capitalism. As each individual pursues their own wellbeing, they somehow help the wellbeing of society.

Experts differ over whether the theory works in the field of economics. But one thing is beyond doubt. The attitude which says that I am an autonomous individual, with a right to pursue my personal goals and insist on personal freedoms, has stuck. To put this in the terms of earlier chapters, individualism marks a full-scale denial of the Christian view that I am essentially a person in relationship. Instead, it claims that I find myself in myself, by digging inside my own solitary brain, by pursuing my own solitary goals.

The underlying individualism of our culture has profoundly coloured the way we view the whole of life, including sex – before, during and after marriage.

If the supreme value is personal freedom, then traditional limitations on sexuality could only be viewed negatively by the permissives of the '60s. There is no earthly reason why, in a sane society, constraints should be seen as negative. The constraint of a lifejacket keeps us afloat. The constraint of walls keeps in heat and keeps out burglars. But when contraception and abortion became widely available in the 1960s, few young adults stopped to ask if the walls so carefully built around sexuality for centuries might in fact have been protective walls. All that mattered was that they were constraints, and constraints were bad. Any limitations had to be a blasphemy against the hallowed idol of personal freedom.

Despite the growing emphasis on individual liberty, until the '60s one compelling reason to exercise sexual restraint was still in place: the risk of pregnancy. And with contraception and abortion that risk was now largely done away with. The shift in the practice of sex outside a permanent, committed relationship was dramatic. In 1965, a third of all 18-year-old boys in the UK, and 17 per cent of girls, had had sexual intercourse. And these figures included those 18-year-olds who were already married! In the short period between 1965 and 1977, these figures had rocketed to 69 per cent, and 55 per cent respectively. By 1994 a large-scale, authoritative survey was showing that only 1 per cent of UK men and 4 per cent of women were virgins on their wedding day.

In the space of not much more than a decade, sex was shifted from the category of delayed gratification to instant gratification. At a stroke wonder died because, unknown to the moral anarchists of the '60s, the walls they had so gleefully kicked down did have a purpose. And this purpose was to preserve wonder. It was to keep it special, to keep it as something to be anticipated with bated breath.

The effects of the '60s libertarian revolution were a little like bludgeoning Santa Claus to death during Advent in order to get at your presents immediately – an act of impatience which ruins the whole point of the exercise and spoils the fun for everybody. But the issue at stake was presented as one of personal freedom, that Pied Piper who must be followed wherever he might lead. And in the case of Baby Boomers, he led directly to the divorce court.

Over the coming two decades, Britain will have to build an additional 4.4 million new homes, to cope with all the homeless singles created by the nation's spiralling divorce rate, the highest in Europe. Between 1971 (when the Divorce Reform Act came into force) and 1990, the divorce rate more than doubled. Official figures released in 1996 warned that unless something drastic happened, 41 per cent of the UK marriages begun that year were likely to end in divorce. In the USA, almost half of all Xers are from broken homes.

As a pastor, sometimes having to minister to people in difficult situations, I know only too well that crude generalizations about people's lives are dangerous. Divorce is rarely something undertaken glibly, and is frequently the result of extreme pressures on a couple from outside – often due to factors such as money and housing. But one thing still needs to be said clearly. The high divorce rate is in large part due to our culture's uncritical bowing before the idol of personal freedom. To the Boomer, personal goals are primary and people secondary. People are more a means to an end than an end in themselves. The attitude which spawned the '60s permissive society – the claim that what matters most is my personal fulfilment, my freedom to chose, my 'rights' – was carried over into marriage.

Marriage was subtly redefined in the popular mind, from something which gives me obligations towards another person to something which meets my emotional and sexual 'needs'. Vows have been subtly redefined, from a binding covenant to an optimistic ideal. It is increasingly taken for granted that 'for better, for worse' means 'for as long as you bring me satisfaction, and unless I find somebody better'. This might sound like an exaggeration, and an unduly harsh judgment. But it is an attitude – expressed in different ways – which I regularly hear voiced by countless young adults. Not least, it is reflected in their increasing reluctance to take on the commitments of marriage at all. By 1994, for the first time ever, more UK couples under 30 were choosing to cohabit rather than marry.

In such a climate, people will go to great lengths to avoid blaming themselves for problems in marriage. If I am ultimately the centre of my own concerns, it follows that I will defend my corner and assert my own rightness. To this end, our culture has latched onto the idea of 'incompatibility' between partners. This passes the blame for relationship breakdown from ourselves to some basic flaw in the marriage. The catastrophic result is that faced with antagonism in a relationship, we tend not to confront our own failings, but to end the marriage, claiming it is 'beyond repair'. Time and again I have seen a person abandon one marriage and soon after start another, without ever asking what it was in them that might have contributed to the ending of the first. Sure enough, the same patterns of behaviour reappear in the second, the third and so on. Individualism whispers that we are never to blame, that we can always pass the buck, and it discourages us from addressing our own destructive tendencies and shortcomings.

Commitment to relationships is on the decline. And yet, in a culture which has opened Pandora's Box of condoms, sex is ubiquitous. In one short journey from my home in North London to the city centre, I walk past several hundred overt images and messages of sexuality. On magazine racks, on billboards, on posters in the Underground, in newspapers, in shop windows, on the increasingly explicit cards in phone boxes, on T-shirts, on commercial radio. Even the children's slide in the park near our home is sometimes decorated with used contraceptives. Urban and suburban life in the West whispers, shouts and screams sex almost incessantly. The inheritance of Xers is to live lives emotionally numbed but sexually aroused.

But some of the people who helped kill off the wonder of sexuality were conservative Christians. In reacting against the sexual excesses of an individualistic culture, what some Christians have offered in its place has been a disaster. Some churches have picked up on one particular anti-sex strand from church history and taught that the physicality of human beings and our capacity for sexuality are somehow wrong. This anti-body, anti-erotic stance would be laughable, had its consequences not been so devastating, since this is the exact opposite of the biblical perspective.

In the biblical understanding, God creates the physical human body as the pinnacle of creation. God makes embodied humanity in his own image, and declares us 'very good'

49

(Genesis 1.31). Part of the creational design for humanity was to be in relationship, and a crucial way this should be expressed is in sex. This fact needs to be underlined, since there is so much nonsense talked about sex being a result of the fall of humankind. Not a bit of it. The new creation was teeming with sexual activity long before it rebelled against the Creator. And this included animals, 'God blessed them and said, "Be fruitful and increase in number" ' (Genesis 1.22), and humans: 'God blessed them and said to them, "Be fruitful and increase in number; fill the earth" ' (Genesis 1.28).

The Creator whose motivation in creating people was love has now made us for love, a love which includes our sexuality. Often the anti-sex brigade have been motivated by a bad theology which carves life up into the opposing poles of sacred and secular, physical and spiritual, which elevates the one and despises the other. Such a distorted, bifocal perspective on the body is a travesty of historic Christianity. Biblical faith affirms the goodness of the physical creation, the body and sexuality, and says we can only find identity in relationship. One of the books of the Bible (the Song of Solomon) is an erotic poem full of explosive *double-entendre*; the heart of the faith is the incarnation ('taking flesh') of God himself, and the Christian vision of eternity is of the resurrection of the physical body.

It is bad enough that this kind of bifocal Christianity has fundamentally distorted Christian teaching on sex and the human body. But the consequences for a generation losing its relational grip has been devastating.

We have a generation pulling back from vulnerability, a generation which has learned emotional numbness as a strategy of survival, and is afraid of long-term commitment. It is a generation relationally stunted, but at the same time sexually sated. It is a generation which has on both counts – emotional and sexual – lost the wonder of personal intimacy. Xers have pushed personal relationships to the top of the agenda, yet our culture can only offer even more individualism and yet more commitment-free sex. The downward spiral merely accelerates.

A radically new vision of relational intimacy is needed, one which attacks the whole charade at its very roots. Such a vision is offered by a Christianity which is fundamentally relational, sexual and offering intimacy. It is this vision which we shall go on to explore in the next chapter. But the vision has been blurred and even obscured in churches which have been fearful of the body, for whom even talk of sex is taboo, and which have seen our embodied natures as somehow less ideal than disembodied 'spirituality'.

Young people soon realize that the attitudes embodied in such churches are not for them, and they give up on them in disgust. They then opt for the only other options available in society, the casual sexuality pushed in every branch of the media and assumed in much sex education. Rightly, these young adults react against a system which seeks to suffocate the body and deny their God-given sexuality. Wrongly, they assume this otherworldly, unbiblical religiosity to represent the entire Christian understanding of sex.

COLLATERAL DAMAGE: THE DEATH OF FRIENDSHIP

When the protective walls around sex are flattened, this not only makes for bad morality, it also makes for bad sex. But there was another victim trampled in the general stampede. The art of non-sexual intimacy between the sexes has particularly suffered.

A good many women my own age choose gay men as their closest male friends. One of these women, Mary, explained why:

> With most men, there's this sense that you know what they're after. Everything is all about working towards sex. So if they're nice to you or take you out, it's because they want to get you into bed. For most of them, it's as if having sex is just a way of saying 'Thanks for a nice evening'. Sometimes you just lie there and put up with it to get rid of them, and you fake orgasm earlier to get rid of them quicker.

51

But with Dan it's different. Because he's gay we both know there's no possibility of sex. So he's just a really good friend. Somebody I can talk to about everything. Somebody who understands the real me, and isn't just after a grope at the end of an evening.

The Christian author Michele Guinness edited an anthology of writings on male–female relationships, published under the title of *Made for Each Other*. In her introduction to the section on friendship between men and women, she comments that this particular chapter ended up the shortest in the book because it was so hard to find anybody to write on the subject. People in our culture have had frighteningly little experience of non-erotic friendship across the genders. The Canadian writer Ronald Rolheiser makes the same sad observation:

Most people have given up on the ideal of deep life-giving friendships between women and men . . . It is rare. Deep, intimate, chaste heterosexual friendship is no small achievement. We lack for models and are virtual pioneers in this partially uncharted area.[1]

The art of non-sexual intimacy in the West is almost finished, although close friendships, with people of the same gender and across the genders, provide glimpses of the wonder for which intimacy was created.

But for most Xers the wonder has been drained from all relationships. Friendships are failing because affection is treated as little more than foreplay, and sexuality is failing because it is something routine and banal.

IN SEARCH OF LOST WONDER

People made in the image of God cannot live without genuine relational intimacy. In relationships with other people we forge our own identity and are opened up to the wonder of encounter. It should come as no surprise, therefore, that Generation X is a generation crying out in desperation for the intimacy which it has been denied as a birthright. Xers are looking in all sorts of ways. One way is in friendship. But a culture raised defensive and mistrusting of others finds it hard to lower the barriers far enough to show the vulnerability of which life-affirming friendships are made. Others look for intimacy in serial sexual relationships, hoping against hope that the next one will bring the longed-for fulfilment. Another is in cohabitation, hoping that this will provide the stability of marriage without its finality.

Others find it in religious cults, with their promise of communal intimacy. Cults are well placed to capitalize on rootless Xers, who prize belonging above all else. To many young adults, the sacrifice of brain and wallet is worthwhile if their hearts are warmed by a caring community. A religiously illiterate culture, craving intimacy, can easily be led by the emotions, even if they are asked to believe blatant nonsense.

It is no surprise that the generation denied the sexual parameters of the past should be desperately improvising parameters of its own. The most common of these improvised parameters is what is 'normal'. This is one reason for the phenomenal success of women's magazines, and the recent wave of men's magazines, with their endless reader surveys and opinion polls. In the absence of any lasting yardsticks, the only measure of the self is how I compare with what my contemporaries are up to: how many times a week, with how many partners, in how many positions, who's faking what, and how often. The opinion survey is the only morality available to a generation soaked in postmodern relativism.

The Big Problem

However, the big problem is this. Generation X is a generation in rebellion against its inheritance. The rampant, self-seeking ambition which characterizes Boomers is seen to have caused untold damage to families, to the environment and to personal integrity. In this sense, Xers are radicals, calling for a new ethic of co-operation, harmony and intimacy. And this is entirely laudable. The relational vision of Generation X marks a massive step forward in Western civilization. From a biblical perspective, it is a vision far more compatible with the values of the gospel than the individualism of the past few decades – even the past few centuries.

But to have the right ideals is one thing. Making them a reality is quite different. And the dilemma for the Xer is that the only tools she has to hand for building community and intimacy are those bequeathed to her by Baby Boomers: a large slice of individualism, slogans about personal freedom, a pile of opinion polls and an aversion to absolutes. The Xer's emotional numbing and distrust of others leaves him with a gap crying out to be filled by intimacy. But in a culture where sex is aggressively marketed, he can only conceive of accessing this through sex. And the ubiquity of casual sex poisons the possibility of genuine friendship.

THE FAILURE OF THE CHURCHES

An alternative vision of relationships as passionate and compassionate was on offer all along, as it had been for nearly two millennia. But those entrusted with being its guardians largely failed to communicate this vision.

Some theologians saw the revolutionaries smashing the protective walls of sexual intimacy and joined in the free-for-all. Not wanting to be thought old-fashioned, they glibly offered theological rationales for any demolition mob on the rampage. The liberal theology of the '60s and '70s can be seen as a faint halo drawn over Baby Boomer 'me-centredness'. It was a large-scale abdication of integrity which many of us who are church leaders in the '90s now find frankly embarrassing.

On the other hand, those who during this period held onto a more biblical ideal so often couched it in negatives and stern moralizing that anybody with any spark of life and fun automatically rejected it wholesale. Xers know to their cost how boring and unfulfilling casual sex may be. But at least it is not as bad as a grim church service. Conservative churches have only themselves to blame that they failed to communicate a biblical vision for sex to post-war young adults. It takes a quite extraordinary degree of skill to take a vision of satisfying, wonder-filled sex, and the possibility of intimate, committed friendship, and make it all sound miserable. But that is precisely what many pastors, nuns and youth workers somehow achieved.

SOMETHING TO CELEBRATE?

A characteristic of my own denomination, the Church of England, is its pastoral sensitivity. While some Christian traditions come across to the watching world as harsh and inflexible, the Anglican Church takes the cultural context of its hearers with utmost seriousness. Perhaps this is in part because its very roots are culturally relative. Formed at the time of the European Reformation, the Church of England was set up with the aim of applying the timeless truths of the gospel to the specific setting of the English nation and people. For a church to be culturally attuned to the people around it is no shame. It is a strength.

It also carries a danger, however. The culturally-attuned church could become the culturally captive church, a church so pastorally sensitive to its people that it ceases to offer any sort of challenge. Towards the end of 1995 the Church of England published a report, *Something to Celebrate*, which surveyed family life in the UK and offered comments and suggestions on current trends. True to Anglican form, it acknowledges accurately and sensitively current trends in family and society, noting the massive changes which have taken place. The report rightly notes the general abandonment of the idea that intercourse presupposes a lifetime commitment. It rightly notes the massive variety of household types now on offer.

The authors go on, however, to suggest that Christians need to develop a 'new sexual ethic' to keep in step with the times, that many singles 'do not feel called to celibacy', and that not to affirm the whole variety of sexual arrangements presently on offer will make the Christian gospel out of touch with today's world. The unspoken assumption behind these claims is that culture leads and gospel follows. If our ideals fail to match the reality, so much the worse for our ideals.

To follow this path, and mould our vision to celebrate the cultural climate, whatever it may be, is actually problematic, even uncaring. The Church is called to be prophetic as well as pastoral. Prophecy is not primarily about predicting the future. It is the art of confronting one's own culture with a vision it has lost. It is the art of truth-telling, even when that truth might be unpopular. It is an art perfected in the wild, restless poetic visions of Isaiah, Jeremiah and the other prophets of ancient Israel.

To be pastoral is to affirm where people are. But what if where they are is partly the result of commercial manipulation, destructive individualism, damaged childhoods, the lies their culture has told them about sex, and their own emotional numbing? What if people are not simply free agents, as Western individualism has assumed, but also victims? What if we live in a culture of addiction, in which many people act not out of freely-made, rational choices, but as slaves to chemical addictions and destructive patterns of compulsive behaviour? Drug-taking, pornography and masturbation, gambling, alcohol abuse, shopping and spending, Internet surfing. The list of obsessive cravings which can grip us and hold us victim is long and growing ever longer.

To adopt a pastoral mode at the expense of the prophetic is to conspire with the spirit of the age and to turn a blind eye to the hopes and lives it is destroying. It is to shake hands with a compulsive, damaging culture and to say it was right all along. To bless the sexual choices of our culture and suggest we reshape our ethics accordingly is equivalent to telling the alcoholic he can have that extra Scotch if he believes it will make him feel calmer and the bulimic that she has every right to vomit if it improves her self-image.

On the other hand to be prophetic without a loving, pastoral heart is to become isolated from people's real-life situations, and to appear judgmental.

Ultimately, those motivated by a vision alien from that of our postmodern consumer culture must be at the same time defiantly prophetic and lovingly pastoral. Without a genuine love, we forego the right and the means to offer hope to confused Xers. But without a prophetic vision, we abandon hope itself.

CHAPTER FOUR

SEX (PART TWO): THE WONDER OF INTIMACY RENEWED

> There are actually many females in the world, and some of them are very beautiful. But where could I find again a face whose every feature, even every wrinkle, is a reminder of the greatest and sweetest memories of my life? Even my endless pains, my irreplaceable losses, I read in your sweet countenance.
>
> Karl Marx, *Letter to his wife*

WONDERFUL SEX, WONDERFUL FRIENDSHIP

Exactly what was trampled in the lemming-rush of 1960s liberalism? Essentially, it was the wisdom that sex is something so precious, something so wonderful, that walls are needed to preserve the wonder. And that these protective walls were there not to stop sex being fun and fulfilling, but precisely to guarantee that it is.

Some walls, such as the Berlin Wall, are to restrict freedom and happiness. Other walls, such as the walls of a bank vault, are to safeguard something precious. Still other walls, such as the walls of a family home, are to protect small children against the wind, the rain and those who would violate their vulnerability. The sexual revolution of the '60s thought it was demolishing a

Berlin wall. It turns out to have been smashing vaults and homes, leaving precious, vulnerable things undefended. Generation X ought to be furious with their forebears. But since these same forebears bequeathed Xers their whole worldview of individualism and self-fulfilment – and since the guardians of a real alternative either threw in the towel, or else made their good news sound like bad news – little of an alternative vision has been on offer.

But there is an alternative vision for sexuality and relationship. A radical, biblical vision. And this vision can be summarized in three statements:

* Alone I am incomplete.

* A partner is subject not object.

* Real sex equals real commitment.

Clearly, the first two points apply both to sexual and non-sexual relationships, and the third just to sexual ones. In a way, each of these statements sounds innocuous, even obvious. But each in its own way is a bombshell for those reared with a limp, post-'60s worldview. Taken together, all three represent a radical, countercultural manifesto of sexuality for the third millennium, with roots planted deep in the wisdom of centuries.

ALONE I AM INCOMPLETE

The first point of our radical sexual vision is shared by both Christians and Xers. Together, they affirm the essentially social nature of personhood. Both the Bible and the gut feelings of a numbed generation tell us that we are incapable of finding identity in isolation from other people. I am inescapably a being in relation.

But to affirm this is to deny the whole philosophical basis of Western culture for the past 400 years. The philosopher Descartes locked the West into radical individualism when he reflected that once everything else has been doubted, the one thing I cannot doubt is that I am an autonomous individual, with my own mental processes: 'I think, therefore I am.' The 18th-century Enlightenment celebrated the rational thought processes of the individual. The 18th- and 19th-century Romantic movement celebrated the emotions of the isolated individual (the precursor of Romanticism, Rousseau, wrote a book entitled *Rêveries of the Solitary Walker* and gave up his own children to an orphanage). The 1960s celebrated the sexual freedom of the individual and the power of the individual to forge their own destiny. The leading exponent of such thinking, the Existentialist writer Jean-Paul Sartre, grimly reflected that *l'enfer, c'est les autres* – hell is other people. The 1980s celebrated the earning-power of the individual, with Margaret Thatcher denying that 'society' even existed.

Not since the Middle Ages has the West been dominated by a relational ideal, which says that people are inescapably bound together, that identity is essentially social. It took our pushing of individualism to the ludicrous extremes of rampant consumerism, the death of sex, the loss of friendship and the destruction of community and the earth before we realized that something was fundamentally wrong. It took all this before we finally began to take issue with the individualist cry that personal freedom was to be valued above all else.

Xers are the first generation to want to make a break with a lonely, failed past, and this is seen by their orientation towards groups and communities rather than individuals. They reject the Boomer lifestyle which says that personal goals and ambitions are central, and that other people are primarily a means to achieving those ends. They have a greater sense of their place in an international community, and enjoy the cultural diversity of 'world music'; they tend to reject the 'ladder' model of careers in favour of jobs which foster relationships and help others; they have a greater concern for marginal groups in society and see multiculturalism as normal; they prize friendships, perhaps as an alternative to failed families. There is evidence that to

Xers, the experience of school is more to do with relationship than achievement – relationship with a peer group, but also with their parents. Xers themselves are less concerned about achievement, but they know for their parents' generation this is the primary goal. So they are anxious to achieve – not so much for themselves as to please their parents. Even dating is done less in the manner of an older generation, by pairing off to the exclusion of others, than in larger groups with other friends.

The shift from individualism to relationship is an exciting vision, a colossal undertaking. But all their role models belong to the enemy camp! Even as Xers start to think about the restoration of community and relationship, the very patterns of thought by which they approach the issues are those handed on by the culture they despise. It is as if a pacifist is handed a machine gun and told to fight for his cause.

Where can Xers look to find solid support for their instincts? The answer lies in the only vigorous, viable tradition of their culture which is fundamentally relational: biblical Christianity, that good news which has so often been packaged to look like bad news.

The heart of the biblical vision for relationships is that we are not designed to be alone. It is alien to our nature to forge an identity alone, to live alone, to reflect alone, to worship alone, to work alone. We discussed in Chapter 2 the insight that to be made in the image of God is firstly to be made in the image not of an isolated, lonely deity, but in the image of one who is already a community of persons. And this community of persons is himself surrounded by a host of other living, responding beings. People sometimes treat the statement, 'God is love' as though it were a meaningless cliché, but the implications of the claim are staggering. It means that the central, underlying principle of the universe is not survival, chaos or chance, but intimate relationship. We were made from love and for love.

That is why the Bible offers examples of intense, committed, non-erotic friendship, including David and Jonathan, Ruth and Naomi, Paul and Timothy, Jesus and John. The instinct towards friendship and companionship is not icing on the cake of life – pleasant but ultimately unnecessary. It is the cake itself. The instinct towards all relationship, but particularly with the opposite gender, is a yearning for wholeness. Without it I am incomplete. When the builders of the tower of Babel had aspirations to godlike status, their punishment was to find their language – the vehicle of communication and intimacy – confused, and their community scattered across the face of the earth (Genesis 11.1–9). In biblical terms, relationship is blessing, individualism a curse.

For this reason, the biblical vision places a strong emphasis on getting love right. Paul's great poem of love in his first letter to the Christians in the ancient city of Corinth – a city well used to casual, loveless sex of every variety – offers a checklist for real intimacy, after underlining the centrality of love:

> If I speak in the tongues of men and of angels, but have not love, I am only a resounding gong or a clanging cymbal. If I have the gift of prophecy and can fathom all mysteries and all knowledge, and if I have a faith that can move mountains, but have not love, I am nothing. If I give all I possess to the poor and surrender my body to the flames, but have not love, I gain nothing.
>
> Love is patient, love is kind. It does not envy, it does not boast, it is not proud. It is not rude, it is not self-seeking, it is not easily angered, it keeps no record of wrongs. Love does not delight in evil but rejoices with the truth. It always protects, always trusts, always hopes, always perseveres. (1 Corinthians 13.1–7)

In this relational, biblical vision there is a particular role for the Christian church as a body of believers. In the Bible, 'church' refers not so much to buildings or liturgies as to people. And the particular calling of that body of people is to embody the love which is to bring hope, healing and intimacy to the world.

62

Our individualistic culture has taught us to view churchgoing as something an individual chooses to do because it brings him personal satisfaction or personal meaning, an alternative to dry-slope skiing or stamp-collecting. It is a lifestyle option. We live in a culture where Baby Boomers see nothing wrong with compulsive 'church-hopping' to find the best 'show' on offer each week. This is far removed from the New Testament model of church as intimate commitment to a community of people.

Some churches express this in terms of 'sacrament' – a concrete, visible embodiment of an invisible and spiritual reality. The definitive sacrament is Jesus of Nazareth, God in human flesh. St Paul writes of the coming of Christ as a *mysterion* (Romans 16.25), a Greek word which translates into Latin as 'sacramentum'. Paul means not that the sacrament of Christ is a mystery in the sense of something hidden or unsolved, but in the sense that something hidden is being revealed. The loving character of God is seen and made real in the person of Jesus.

But after the death and resurrection of Christ, the sacrament of God's presence on earth is the church, because it constitutes the 'body of Christ'. All Paul's reflections on love in 1 Corinthians 13 are understood in the context of Chapter 12 of the same letter, where he tells the young church that together they are a single body (v. 12), which is the body of Christ on earth (v. 27). And that if they take the body analogy seriously, they will realize that each part is vital for the working of the whole, that each has a distinct role to play in the functioning of the body (vv. 14–26). There can be no such thing as a solitary believer. A person is only a believer in so far as they are a part of the sacramental body of Christ on earth, the body of people gripped by the gospel. And when Paul tells the same audience, 'Don't you know that you yourselves are God's temple . . . ?' (1 Corinthians 3.16), the Greek for 'you' is plural. It is together, not individually, that they constitute the holy sanctuary where God himself makes his home.

According to historic Christianity, the instincts of Xers are right: I am incomplete alone. Identity is relational, the basis of our survival and wellbeing is relational, and our faith is inescapably relational too. Xers, in rebellion against Baby Boomer individualism, are already halfway to the gospel.

A PARTNER IS SUBJECT NOT OBJECT

The fatal flaw in Western individualism has been in seeing each person as the sun at the centre of their own solar system. Alone, splendid, autonomous, but surrounded by a number of dependent planets.

This view shaped, and was in turn shaped by, many of the great thinkers and movements of the past two centuries. Darwin gave rise to the belief that life is a struggle for individual survival, if necessary at the expense of others. Intimacy is merely a useful device for propagating one's own line.

The rise of post-war consumerism told us that only individual fulfilment mattered, that the goal of life was prosperity. That vision, under the name of the American Dream, has urged on the aspirations of a now global culture.

Those of us who are Boomers breathe an air of rampant individualism. And it would be astonishing if this had not shaped our attitudes to relationships. The result, usually unconsciously held, has been an attitude which says: 'I am a subject. Other people are objects.' People are of interest to me in so much as they contribute towards my own goals of self-fulfilment and happiness. I relate in order to meet my emotional needs. I parent in order to express my parenting instinct. That which ought to undercut individualism – relationship – is co-opted into the service of personal autonomy. I have my rights to certain things, and others are there to help me achieve them.

The problem for Xers is that there is no other air to breathe. They inhale consumer individualism simply by being alive. Once again, however, the assumptions of the culture are flatly contradicted by the Christian gospel. Other people are not objects, defined only in relation to myself. They are not there to meet my 'needs', bring me personal fulfilment, or be my rivals in the battle for survival.

An encounter with another person is an encounter with that which is truly 'other' than myself. That person has her own story, her own place in God's big story, and her own network of defining relationships which bring her a stable, unique identity all of her own. When we meet another person, befriend another person, make love to another person, our response should be one of astonishment and wonder at their sheer difference from ourselves.

In our society the main causes of breakdown in relationship – taking people for granted, boredom, disagreements and physical violence – all stem from the mistaken expectation that the real reason other people are around is to help me through life. In essence, it stems from a lack of respect and awe before the other. It is only when we ditch this basic assumption that real, mutual relationship starts to become possible.

To love the world and be committed to the welfare of all people everywhere is easy. To love and be committed to one other person is the real test of our love. We can swear our boundless devotion to the wellbeing of all humanity. But we do not have to put up with all humanity sitting at our dinner table, sleeping in our bed, and leaving their socks under our sofa.

Humankind is so vague as to be undemanding. 'Humanity' is a product of our own creation – based on stereotypes, holiday snaps and media reports. It is easy to love that which is a projection of our own mind, that which we can control. But a close friend or a lover demands more than to be an object of benevolence. They demand intimacy, which is a meeting of two subjects in a context of mutual awe and respect.

Every intimate friendship and every expression of our sexuality is a re-enactment of the primal encounter of one human subject with another. Particularly in male–female encounter, we each stand in the same place as Adam and Eve. The Canadian writer Mike Mason writes movingly, in his book *The*

Mystery of Marriage, that this primary encounter with similarity-yet-otherness is at the heart of our sexuality:

> For secretly we long to perpetuate that one astounding moment in the Garden of Eden. We long to stand in awe of one another, just as Adam and Eve must have done when they first locked gazes. We long for our whole body to tingle with the thrill of knowing that this one fascinating being, this being of a different gender, has been created especially for us and given to us unreservedly for our help, comfort and joy. Men and women ache for the heart with which to know this reality, and for the eyes with which to see one another (and therefore themselves) as the astounding miracles that they are.[1]

This is the quality of intimacy for which we are created, and we remain incomplete until it is ours. The casual holiday fling, the fast-food shag, the thank-you-and-goodnight bonk are not intimacy. They do not even come close. And people wonder why these experiences leave them feeling empty and unsatisfied. Such relationships are in reality acts of abuse. Abuse means using another for my personal goals or satisfaction, irrespective of their dignity.

It is this crucial insight, of intimacy as a meeting of awe-struck equals, that is behind Jesus's insistence that we should love another *as we love ourselves* (Matthew 22.39). In a society of individualists, that is no easy task. It involves a degree of selflessness for which our culture has not prepared us. Intimacy with another might open me up to an extraordinary degree of wholeness and satisfaction; but it also opens me up to an extraordinary level of pain and misunderstanding. The best part of intimacy, the 'otherness' of the other, is also its most agonizing quality. Intimacy, that piquant blend of intense love and potential hurt, is challenging. But to fail to rise to the challenge is forever to accept second best.

Mike Mason says the central act of intimacy is contemplation. I gaze on another person, filled with wonder that some-

thing so similar to myself can at the same time be so impene-
trably mysterious. I am encountered by the mystery of life from
beyond my own horizons. And as I engage intimately with
another I contemplate the very image of God before my eyes.
Some claim that we are closer to God in a garden than any-
where else on earth, but in the mystery of human relationships
we come closer to God than is possible in even the most sub-
lime scene of natural beauty. In close friendship and in sexual
intimacy, two alien worlds meet and stare open-mouthed at
each other, amazed to find that they are not alone, amazed at
finding intelligent life where none was expected.

REAL SEX EQUALS REAL COMMITMENT

The previous two points have applied as much to friendship as
to sexual relationships. Is there, then, no significant difference
between the two? Does it follow that any relationship in which
we find personal identity and wholeness, and where there is
genuine awe and wonder before the other, may be expressed
erotically? To answer this, we need to look more closely at the
meaning of sex itself.

Western culture today prides itself on being holistic, on inte-
grating all the varied facets of the human make-up. Not for us
the otherworldliness of Victorian piety, or the rationalism of
Enlightenment thought. Our culture believes it has rediscovered
the physical body, the earth, spirituality, the power of the
feminine and the insights of native cultures. And yet, in the
area of sexuality, our culture is the least holistic that has ever
existed. We have learned to live as if we can split off the physical aspect of our make-up from all the others.

Body, mind and spirit belong together. To be holistic is to
insist that all three step in time, and that one does not run off
ahead of the rest. Postmodern thought rightly accuses the
dominant Western intellectual traditions of allowing one aspect
– mind – free rein, whilst playing down the body. In the same
way, liberation theologians rightly accuse the dominant

Western religious traditions of ignoring the radical challenge of Christianity to political and social structures.

But somehow sex is different. We behave as if we can say with our naked bodies what we would not say with our mind, emotions, or words. Sexual intimacy says with my body: I love you; I give myself wholly to you; I am committed to you. I am exposing the deepest, most intimate parts of my very being to you, even as I expose the deepest, most intimate parts of my unclothed body to you. And this is emphatically not something culturally relative, as if native peoples walk around blasé about nakedness. Anthropologists will tell you that such people in fact have extremely sophisticated categories of dress and undress. The ways they express these categories are different from ours, certainly, and might involve little more than a slim thong around the waist, but they are very real nonetheless. We too instinctively know the difference between a girl wearing a skimpy bikini and lying totally naked on the beach, even though there may be little objective difference between the two.

The physical nakedness of sexual intimacy is about baring our soul to another. It is about vulnerability and absolute surrender. It is about opening up the hidden, private areas of our selves, both literally and metaphorically. Mike Mason again:

> Exposure of the body in a personal encounter is like the telling of one's deepest secret: afterwards there is no going back, no pretending that the secret is still one's own or that the other does not know. It is, in effect, the very last step in human relations, and therefore never one to be taken lightly. It is not a step that establishes deep intimacy, but one which presupposes it.[2]

In other words, sexual intercourse says: 'This is absolute self-giving. I can give you no more of myself than this complete intimacy. This is the level of surrender which is appropriate because ours is a permanent, committed relationship.' If Mason is right, and I believe he is, this has massive implications for a generation which reverses the process and, far from seeing sex as the ultimate point of intimacy, sees it as a casual starting point which might or might not lead to intimacy.

One implication is that it diminishes our integrity as persons, since sex outside a context of trust and permanence – as in casual sex or adultery – is the art of telling lies. It is saying physically what I could never say in words: 'I commit myself to you absolutely, permanently, vulnerably.'

Another implication of all this for our culture is that it downgrades the quality of sex. Experts are constantly telling us that good sex is not primarily about technique. It is about trust and openness, and it takes a very long time to get it right. Indeed, it takes years of embarrassment, mistakes, and a context of good communication – and a sense of humour! – to get it right. These are all the factors which are absent in casual sex. Time is short, communication minimal, and trust non-existent. All the preconditions of good sex are missing. We are raising a generation of bad lovers. If biblical Christianity insists that sex needs to be protected by boundary walls, it is in part to maintain the quality of sex.

Interestingly, surveys reveal that the people in Western culture who have the most active sex lives, and with the highest rate of regular orgasms, are conservative Christians. An authoritative survey of the sex life of Americans from 1994 backs this up.[3] The researchers asked women whether they 'always' experienced sexual climax during lovemaking. Of those who claimed no religious affiliation, 22 per cent agreed that they did. The figure for conservative Protestant women was considerably higher, at 32 per cent. The study also found that conservative Protestant men and women lead all other groups, religious and non-religious, in the frequency of sexual intercourse.

Christian sex has had a bad press down the centuries. But an examination of history shows that the sexually active conservative Protestants of the USA are no aberration. Their Puritan forebears, despite their largely undeserved reputation as world-deniers, wrote long and enthusiastically about sexuality and intimacy as divine blessings. Indeed, the Puritans' positive approach to sexuality was a cultural turning-point for Western culture in that it overturned the earlier medieval glorification of celibacy. When one New England Puritan husband refused to have sex with his wife, their church excommunicated him.[4]

Another implication of seeing fast-food sex as the norm is an unlearning of the language of touch. When it becomes second nature to see touch as a precursor to sex, its subtlety is lost. The language of touch is almost as dead as Latin and Sanskrit. To a contemporary audience, the novels of Jane Austen and the early movies of Hollywood might be products of another universe. All that seething passion expressed in the touch of a finger, a single kiss, the casual brush against a person's side. Such novels and films speak with a whole vocabulary of touch most of us have never been taught. Especially for those of us with an Anglo-Saxon heritage, only two options are open: a complete absence of touch as we each defend our own private 'space', or else full intercourse. It is as if we have learned a language in which the only registers are silence and screaming yourself hoarse.

Sex therapists tell us that the results of our illiteracy in the language of touch have been catastrophic for the quality of our lovemaking when it does occur, and that contemporary men are especially inept in this area. The sex therapists Dr David Delvin and Christine Webber conducted a major sex survey, in which they asked women respondents to state the advice they would most like to give their male partners.[5] The overwhelming answer came back: 'Tell them to take their time!' The authors cite a survey of Scottish women which shows they would like a full hour of gentle touch before even thinking about climax. A similar survey of American women requests between 15 and 45 minutes. Delvin and Webber quote the complaint of many women correspondents: 'My man only touches and kisses me when he wants sex.' The message to the woman in such cases is clear: touch and kissing are only a prelude to the bedroom. The idea that these things might be ends in themselves, low-key expressions of affection, has largely been lost amongst men today.

Another implication of letting your body speak louder than your commitments is the loss of wonder in relationships. For years my wife and I had wanted to go for the most spectacular meal imaginable – irrespective of cost – just to see what the experience would be like. Since our student days in Oxford we had driven wistfully past the entrance to the Manoir aux Quat' Saisons many times. The Manoir is no ordinary restaurant. It is the home of the internationally famous French chef Raymond Blanc, well-known for turning eating into a fine art form.

After 11 years of waiting and longing, I finally decided to take the plunge and secretly booked a table for two for my wife's 30th birthday. The price of the meal was enough to make the strongest man go weak at the knees. The combination of all the years of waiting and the exorbitant price made every tiny morsel a precious thing, every mouthful was savoured at length, every inch of the room's décor studied with appreciation.

Some will tell me we wasted our money. Some will tell me how many burgers or helpings of fish and chips that money would have bought. But that would be to miss the point. There was something immeasurably precious and perfect about that evening. It said something about the wonder of fine cuisine, something fast-food devotees will never understand, and it said something about the wonder of my relationship with my wife.

When we insist that sex is so precious it needs strong walls built around it, we say something about the wonder of intimacy that the fast-food sex junkies will never understand either. They look on and actually feel sorry for us. They think that because we want to keep sex special, we are anti-sex. If it wasn't so tragic, the scale and the irony of their incomprehension would be rather funny.

CITY OF CASUAL SEX

If Xers were to travel back in time to the ancient world and look for common points of reference, one of the cities where they would feel most at home would be the Greek city of Corinth. It was the commercial gateway between the thriving cultures of Italy and Asia, it was an economic boom-town, with a populace from all around the known world. Because of its cosmopolitan make-up, it was a centre where the culture, thinking and religions of the West mixed with mystery cults from the East. Its strategic position, its commercialism and pluralism of cultures and creeds anticipated the multicultural cities of today: London, New York, Los Angeles, Toronto, Sydney.

Today's young adults would have recognized much in the Corinthians' attitude to sexuality. As a commercial seaport, Corinth gained such a reputation for free and easy sex that one ancient writer, Aristophanes, used the term 'act like a Corinthian' to mean 'to fornicate'. Many in Corinth saw sex as no more meaningful than a quick snack – a way of satisfying a bodily appetite, with no deeper significance. The apostle Paul had friends in Corinth, and so it was natural that they should express the widespread view of their day about sex by quoting to him some of the popular sayings of their culture: 'Everything is permissible for me', 'Food for the stomach and the stomach for food'. In other words, sex is what the body is there for. Let's get on and do it.

We know Paul's friends were quoting such sayings to him, because in a letter he quotes these proverbs back at them, before going on to offer his own thoughts on the issue (1 Corinthians 6.1–20). In his reply, Paul underlines a point which would have been familiar to anybody familiar with the teachings of Jesus and Judaism, but quite alien to the lifestyle in Corinth. It is the idea that the act of sex makes two people into 'one flesh' (v. 16). This notion of 'one flesh' goes back to the Genesis creation accounts:

The man said,
'This is now bone of my bones
and flesh of my flesh;
she shall be called 'woman',

for she was taken out of man.'
For this reason a man will leave his father and mother and
be united to his wife, and they will become one flesh.
  (Genesis 2.23, 24)

The same image is underlined and reinforced by Jesus:

'Haven't you read,' he replied, 'that at the beginning the
Creator "made them male and female", and said, "For this
reason a man will leave his father and mother and be united
to his wife, and the two will become one flesh"? So they are
no longer two, but one. Therefore what God has joined
together, let not man separate.' (Matthew 19.4–6)

From Genesis to Paul, via Jesus, the same message is given. We
cannot split off the language spoken by our bodies from that
spoken by our mouths. Sexual intercourse surrenders the body
totally to one other person. It says 'This act is so utterly powerful in its power to bind and unite that we are now no longer
two but one.' According to the biblical story, casual, commitment-
free sex is a contradiction in terms. It simply cannot exist. Every
act of sex is a declaration of covenant, or a binding statement
of commitment and surrender to that one special person. In the
context of the Christian story, extramarital intercourse is in
effect impossible, since by having sex you have already given
the fullest statement of commitment and surrender anybody
could ever give to another person.

This exclusive relationship which gives the context for full
sexual intimacy is characterized by fidelity, trust, selflessness,
permanence, surrender, affection and personal maturity. It is
what we know as marriage. Of course, marriage is expressed in
a vast range of cultural forms. And it is surrounded by a huge
variety of family patterns: from the small nuclear family, to the
massive wider family or clan. But the Christian vision insists that
the norms of what we call marriage are not culturally bound,
but God-given and universal. And to stop short of the norms
which characterize marriage is to stop short of a full commitment

to permanence. It is only these norms which offer the rich, dark earth, the moisture and the sunlight which allow the bright, fragrant but delicate flower of sexuality to thrive.

I was brought up in a town near Stratford-upon-Avon, home of Shakespeare and the Royal Shakespeare Company. One of the pleasures of life as a sixth-former was to arrive at the theatre in Stratford on the evening of a performance and buy a cheap 'student standby' ticket. This would allow impoverished enthusiasts such as myself to see the whole performance, standing up. However, I would go secure in the knowledge that by the half-time interval, and sometimes after just 15 minutes, I would be seated in one of the best seats of the house. Such seats would be vacated by middle-aged American couples who could be heard to mutter as they left, 'C'mon, honey, let's go check out a movie. That was just so boring.' In one sense, they were right. The movie will give them all the culture and pathos which a sound-bite culture can ask for. In another sense, however, their response was an admission of defeat. They had stopped short of a commitment to see things through to the end. I was the last to complain; their loss was my gain. But I longed to be able to tell them that there might be more to the arts than they had yet experienced, greater subtlety, poetry and nuance, that to stick with it might have helped resensitize them to the possibilities of great drama. Perhaps my ideals were unrealistic. Most people uncritically live out whatever their culture has given them, no matter how limited or impoverishing. But I still hold out the same vision for marriage. It is still possible.

Our culture encourages us to reinterpret relationships in the same way that 'greatest hits' compilations reinterpret classical music: offering the highlights without the boring bits in between. The problem is, the highlights only make sense in the context of the long, seemingly uneventful stretches which join them. To want the highlights in isolation misses the very point of those highlights. We are denying ourselves the full glory, the full subtlety.

To speak of modern sexuality in such terms is not judgmentalism. I should hope that nobody, least of all Christians who believe in a gospel of God's unmerited, free grace, would be judgmental of lifestyle options different from their own. And there is no reason to single out falling short of a sexual ideal as any different from falling short in other, less controversial areas, such as gossip, lack of charity, or judgmentalism itself. But it is a question of whether we live as optimistic visionaries or pessimistic realists.

Fatal Attraction is one of the most powerful movies ever made. Its problem, however, is that it tells the wrong story. It tells of a married man, played by Michael Douglas, who has a sexual fling with an unattached woman, played by Glenn Close. As far as the man is concerned, that is the end of it, but she has other ideas. He attempts to return to normal family life as if nothing has happened, but she will not let it rest. The gory, repulsive ending of the film shows the man and his wife together killing the mistress, who by this stage has become like a crazed animal, and returning to their domestic bliss.

The reason it tells the wrong story is that the mistress is the most sane character in the film. She is the one who knows that the sexual encounter was more than recreational fun. No sex can be casual, but here is a man who pretends it can be. In sex he has spoken a depth of commitment which he never for a moment considered keeping. The real story is left unexplored: the tragedy of a woman, integrated in her selfhood and sexuality, who is the victim of a warped culture.

All this is why the heart of a biblical sexuality is a commitment to fidelity, which is an act of speech, will, body and feelings. This has implications not only in terms of casual sex and adultery, but also for whether a couple decides to stay together or separate. As I was writing this book I learned of yet another couple of acquaintances who are about to divorce. The reason given, as so often, was that one partner was changing, 'finding themselves', and growing away from their spouse. They needed to be 'free' to be the person they 'really' are, and the other partner had become a hindrance to that self-realization.

This is nonsense, based on the almost universally believed, but wholly wrong, idea that we fundamentally 'find ourselves' in isolation, by digging inside our own heads. It assumes that the 'real' me is that autonomous individual who needs to get in touch with my own feelings, my own ambitions, my own priorities.

If we are right to say that we only find our identity in relationship with other people, it is doubly true that we can only find ourselves in the context of the binding commitments we have made to others, spouse and children alike. Simply to opt out is no solution. If my very self is inseparable from the relationships to which I belong, to pull away is not liberation. It is a partial suicide.

REKINDLING THE WONDER

These, then, are the three walls vital to protect the wonder of real intimacy, three parameters which respect our nature as persons in relationship, the dignity of others and the wonder of sexuality:

* Alone I am incomplete.

* A partner is subject not object.

* Real sex equals real commitment.

But in a culture which has lost its grip on intimacy, to talk in such terms might sound wildly idealistic. What can we say to those whose experience is far removed from any such ideals? Specifically, what about:

– those people outside the lifelong committed relationship which most cultures know as marriage;
– those people in a marriage which feels dry and lacking in all wonder;

– and those who feel that their past experiences of casual sex have killed any possibility of wonder?

We shall conclude this chapter by looking briefly at each.

First, those outside a lifetime committed relationship. Our problem in this respect is that we live in a culture which actively discourages personal integrity and maturity in relationships. Personal maturity involves learning the language of intimacy: when to whisper, when to shout, when to remain silent. Different registers are appropriate for different relationships.

For the majority of my casual acquaintances a handshake is sufficient. For close friends – male and female – a warm hug and affectionate touch express that they are worth more to me than somebody I have just met. In relationship with a person with whom I have set up some kind of exclusive partnership, but stopped short of total surrender and permanent commitment, it is right to begin to learn the art of the kiss, the passionate embrace, the sensual touch, but knowing that intercourse is simply not appropriate yet. Why should I learn to become skilled in the art of telling lies, especially to the one with whom I am learning about intimacy and openness?

Many books, particularly aimed at Christian teens, give lists of 'dos' and 'don'ts' in sexuality. It seems to me this rather misses the point, and is in many ways counterproductive. For one thing, human nature is such that on seeing a list of prohibited pleasures, our immediate desire is to try out every single one of them! We ask what is so special about this thing that they are trying to ban us from doing. Secondly, it falls into the same trap as the sex-sated culture of the late 1990s. It discourages maturity in relationships and personal responsibility. It lays down laws, telling you what you ought to be doing, rather than inviting you to reflect on what will help you grow as an integrated, fulfilled person and to discover the role one's sexual and other relationships play in the process of shaping our identity.

So the message to those outside a lifetime covenant relationship is an invitation to intimacy and relationship, no less than to those who are married. But the ways this is expressed will be different. It will involve rediscovering the lost art of vulnerable, self-giving friendship, with people of the opposite sex and the same sex, and rediscovering the touch of affection. Most of all, it will involve learning to be a whole, integrated person, learning the art of cultural resistance in a society which severs body from mind, sexuality from commitment.

There is not space to go into all the issues surrounding sexuality and singleness. Other books offer a fuller treatment of this theme. But our bottom line must be a fundamental challenge to the strange credo of our sexually anarchic culture – its belief that even bad copulation is better than good friendship.

Is there hope for those in a wonderless marriage? If we feel trapped by a relationship which was begun with high ideals and eager vows of commitment, but which now seems arid and life-denying, then is there no hope left?

The reason this type of situation seems hopeless is due to another of our cultural myths. Western thinking has assumed for centuries that what we think and feel shapes what we do. Applied to love, this means that if we have warm and gooey feelings towards the loved one, if we fall in love with them, then we will act on those feelings by carrying out loving actions: sending cards and flowers, buying gifts, holding somebody close, kissing, sharing a candle-lit meal together.

However, it is equally true (although our romance-infatuated culture has kept this a big secret) that what we do shapes what we feel. The point is well made by the sociologist Tony Campolo,[6] who writes that whenever he counsels individuals who claim the romance has gone from their marriage, and that the only course open to them now is to end it, he tells them to do the following:

1) Each day make a new list of ten things that you would do for your spouse if you were in love.

2) Then each day, do the ten things that are on that list.

Campolo's advice for putting the wonder back into intimacy sounds so simple as to be naive. But, as many couples have found, it actually works. And the reason it works is because of one vital truth. That love is not just feeling. It is actions. Love is not a force which overcomes us as we sit passively. It is an act of the will, something we choose to do. Even our fantasy life is an act of the will: fantasy can both draw us outside the committed relationship, or it can help restore the wonder to it. Relationships, like houseplants, die of neglect.

Dave was 37, and had been married for eight years to Jan when he began to notice Sarah. Sarah, who worked in the same office as Dave, was a good ten years younger than Jan, and was single. Was it his imagination, or was she making excuses to walk over to his side of the office whenever she could? He liked the way she laughed, the way her eyes twinkled. When they talked she seemed to understand him in a way Jan rarely did. She made him feel alive in a way he had not felt since the early days of his marriage. Come to think of it, had he ever felt this way about Jan? He was not sure if he had ever really been 'in love' with Jan in this fizzy, heart-stopping way. What had he been missing out on all these years?

Dave had a choice. He could pursue his infatuation with Sarah. He could conclude that he and Jan had grown apart over the years, and that he had a right to the kind of romantic excitement he had so far been denied. In short, he could have an affair. This, in turn, might lead to a divorce from Jan and a magical new life with Sarah.

Or he could laugh at himself, pull himself together and resolve to channel all his desire for romance, love, that new tingle-factor he was experiencing, into his marriage. He could work at falling in love with Jan for the first time. He could woo her, as if she were the most stunning girl he had ever met. And he could keep Sarah as a friend, but knowing that sex with her was simply out of the question. He could invite her and other colleagues home, to meet Jan.

But nobody had ever told Dave that the second option was

an option at all. It remains a secret many people in our culture have never heard. And Dave is a romantic, led by the heart. He had long dreamed of the kind of passionate romance he had seen in the old film *Brief Encounter*. It was natural that he should choose the first option, an affair with Sarah. As a result of the affair, he and Jan separated, although Jan was very reluctant to do so. Shortly afterwards, the bright and bubbly Sarah found a younger man. At the time of writing, Dave's divorce is about to go through, and he now lives alone in a small flat, regularly trawling night-clubs in search of that perfect partner who will make his heart fizz once again.

Instead of keeping both a marriage to Jan and a friendship with Sarah, Dave lost both. Our culture is full of 'Daves' of both sexes, their heads full of the *Brief Encounter* myth: that somewhere, out there, is the perfect partner, the one who will sweep me off my feet with a hitherto unknown passion, that I must follow this passion wherever it might lead. And that once the passion has gone from a marriage, it remains forever bland and beyond salvage; that it is impossible to fall in love with the person you are married to.

The myth is as dangerous as it is all-pervasive. The reality is that romantic and sexual love only really works best in the place it was designed to be enjoyed: a lifelong commitment to one other person. A cold, wonderless marriage can be rekindled into a blaze of thrill and sexual excitement. It happens time after time. It is an exciting reality, but one kept secret by our culture. Houseplants revive when watered and fed. A marriage is revived when partners refuse to allow it to die of neglect and are determined to work at it.

The implications of this for love-jaded Xers are remarkable. It means that wonder in relationships is not something which might or might not drift our way, like a raincloud. It is not a hit or miss affair. Rather, wonder can be rekindled. But it will take time and effort.[7]

Finally, what about those whose past experiences seem to have deadened the wonder of intimacy? What hope for the man who meets the most wonderful girl he could have possibly imagined, and longs to give himself to her fully and for life, but knows he has slept with so many others that intimacy with her will be neither new nor special?

Fortunately, we are not left alone and in despair. The same gospel that offers us an ideal of wonder in relationship also holds out the promise of forgiveness when we smother that wonder, through our ignorance, stupidity or rebellion. Ronald Rolheiser, in his book of meditations *Forgotten Among the Lilies*, calls this healing of past mistakes 'revirginization', the miraculous gift of wonder renewed. It is an experience of new birth, something to which we shall return in the final chapter.

The middle-aged journalist sat opposite me with a twinkle in his eyes. 'You could say I was a bit of a naughty boy in my youth.' He winked and gave me knowing looks. 'I did rather play the field. In a way, it was what people expected of you where I come from. You know: bit of a Jack-the-lad and all that. The trouble was, when I met Jenny I felt sick at all that stuff I'd been doing for all those years. I was convinced that I'd ruined any chance of our sex-life being special, because I'd done it all before, with so many people.

'Anyway, I handed it over to God. I really prayed that he could take away the past and let me start all over again. And do you know, he did. I still regret all that sleeping around, and all the people I must have hurt. That will never go away. But all I know is that on our wedding night, I was like a 15-year-old on his first date. I was really embarrassed, excited, fumbling and hesitant. It was as if I'd never been with any girl ever before.' Like my journalist friend, Generation X longs to be revirginized into wonder.

It is not only those with a history of promiscuity who experience the death of wonder in intimacy. I met Jill when she was on her fourth marriage and had had a history of shorter, intense flings. Each of these relationships had fallen apart, according to Jill, due to 'incompatibility'. It soon became clear, however, that Jill's real problem was this: she was a romance addict. She was using her serial monogamy as an attempt to realize the Technicolor romances of her daydreams. But with each subsequent relationship, the analogies with her bodice-ripping, candle-lit, desert island fantasies seemed to grow ever fainter.

Hope for Jill could never come from the dominant values of our therapeutic culture. She had followed the wide path of immediate personal gratification, only to find that round several bends the path petered out, leading her in a bleak and rocky terrain, more alone than when she started the journey. Jill found, although she still finds it hard to admit this to herself, that her culture lied to her. It told her the big questions of meaning, truth, purpose and goodness were unanswerable and therefore unimportant; that all she could hope for was personal comfort and the thrill of the moment. She believed and pursued this passionately, only to end up finding even this eluding her.

There is hope for Jill. But it must stem from a brutal reassessment of the myths of her culture, myths which told her to forget questions of plot and purpose, to deny even that she was part of a bigger plot at all, and to focus on the details of life. Experience has taught her, the hard way, that such details only find their meaning in a bigger context, that there must be more to life than self-gratification and living for the present. And hope for Jill must come from brutal realism about herself – facing up to the brokenness within her own life, tracing the roots of her compulsions, challenging the unattainable fantasies which have motivated her whole adult life.[8]

Hope for Jill can only come through identifying the lie on which her life has been built, and the unseen forces which have fed her compulsions. It must come from honesty in admitting her complicity with a culture of lies, and from an experience of inner healing of damage done. Jill too can be revirginized. But her revirginization can only come from a brutal reassessment of all she has held dear and a new beginning. It can only come through a kind of rebirth.

INDIGNATION

Many Xers will have read this chapter with the indignation their culture reserves for anybody who challenges its most fundamental assumptions. Even now, many readers are asking, 'What right do you have to tell us how to run our sex-lives? If we're happy with what we're doing, then why can't we get on with it?' The answer, of course, is that I have no right at all to tell anybody how to express their sexuality. But the simple fact is that Xers are not happy with what they are doing.

A whole generation of young adults is doing what it likes, but no longer likes it very much. Xers have found to their cost the emptiness of casual sex, the boredom of commitment-free intimacy, the agonizing loneliness of a life lived without the openness and vulnerability of true friendship. They are longing for a fresh vision.

CHAPTER FIVE

EARTH:
THE WONDER OF
CREATION

At the outset the universe appears packed with will, intelligence, life and positive qualities; every tree is a nymph and every planet a god. Man himself is akin to the gods. The advance of knowledge gradually empties this rich and genial universe: first of its gods, then of its colours, smells, sounds and tastes, finally of solidity itself.

C.S. Lewis, Preface to *The Hierarchy of Heaven and Earth*
by D.E. Harding

OLD MAPS

I love old maps of the world, with their fat-cheeked babies blowing many-masted galleons, their sea-monsters dancing in the foam, their Latin words and obscure planetary diagrams. I love the way the familiar outlines of countries look squashed and misshapen, as if they have been left on a bus and sat upon by a fat man. I try to imagine what it must have felt like, hundreds of years ago, to know that massive tracts of the globe were as yet unexplored, and to imagine what lost cities, vast jungles and serpentine rivers might lie there.

I admit this is a terribly Eurocentric view, and politically incorrect in the extreme. Most 'undiscovered' lands were home to native inhabitants, and 'discovery' in many cases meant bringing the worst aspects of Western culture. All this is true. But the romance of those old maps still lingers, with their promises of new horizons to be explored, new wonders to be found. It is an excitement which emerges in the best contemporary travel writing, sometimes in fantasy fiction. But somehow we seem incapable of recapturing the wonder of those old cartographers as they mapped the earth in all its mysterious glory.

I wonder how one of those map-makers, or an explorer such as Vasco da Gama or Sebastian Cabot, would have reacted to Alan. It was 1994, just after the suicide of Kurt Cobain, singer of the grunge rock band Nirvana and widely heralded as the voice of his generation. We were discussing why young adults were killing themselves in such large and growing numbers. I asked Alan, 19, why he believed there had been such a rash of sympathetic suicides by Cobain's contemporaries across North America and Europe.

He thought for a while. 'It's a lot to do with depression, turning in on yourself. But there's also a sense that there's nothing much worth living for. You've experienced everything life has to offer . . . you've been to lots of places . . . met lots of people . . . and you're still feeling bored and miserable. You know nothing's ever going to change . . . so what's there to stick around for?'

For Alan and many others like him, suicide has become just another lifestyle option for a jaded generation, a last high, a one-way ticket to the only territory still unexplored. For many Xers the real, material world around them is prosaic and ordinary, the banal backdrop to a bored existence.

Such opinions are no longer minor streams in the current thinking of young adults. They have become a powerful torrent. But what are the tributaries which have contributed to the flow? It has been the combination of a number of factors.

THE RISE OF SCIENTIFIC MATERIALISM

One reason for the stripping away of wonder from the earth has been the direction of Western science and technology over the past 300 years. From the late 17th century, under the influence of European thinkers such as Descartes and Newton, people increasingly started to describe the natural world as a machine which ran according to laws of cause and effect. To begin with, this was usually held in tension with a belief in God – sometimes the God of the Bible, sometimes a more distant, shadowy 'First Principle'. If the earth was a complex mechanism, God was the watchmaker.

It was not long before the rise of naturalism, the view that the physical universe is all there is. According to this view, human beings are merely a particularly complex form of machine which has evolved. Even human personality, and emotions such as love, are part of the machine. In the dry worldview of naturalism, the earth is an impersonal commodity to be used and exploited. Those things which provoke wonder in the human psyche – the appreciation of beauty, an encounter of surprise and awe, respect for otherness, the dimension of the spirit – are excluded. Scientific materialism is reductionist – it reduces the rich variety of life to a single track – and among those things which are reduced are the roots of wonder.

THE COMMUNICATIONS REVOLUTION

Another tributary into the current of indifference has been the dramatic boom in communications technology, combined with our ever more sophisticated means of transportation. It is easy to forget just how recently this has come about. I recently spoke to an elderly woman born before Wilbur and Orville Wright designed and flew the first powered aeroplane in 1903, and well before 1926, when John Logie Baird first transmitted moving images. By the end of the same century, we have satellite and cable TV, mobile phones, fax, the Internet, e-mail, FM radio, pagers and a global network of international airports.

Nowhere is really remote and undiscovered any more. We watch in intimate detail the lives of rainforest tribes, foreign royalty and those who live in the snows of Northern Canada.

Television news brings instant images from every part of the globe. I might never have spoken to my next-door neighbour, but I can watch a man in Kiev eating breakfast and chat to somebody in their bath in Toowoomba. Such massive-scale, global communications are an astounding achievement. But the effect has been a little like casual sex. Promiscuous media consumption has a deadening effect on our capacity for awe before the strange and exotic. For us, nothing is new any more. We have been everywhere, seen everybody, done everything.

Virtual Existence

It is not simply that communications saturation has left us indifferent to things which would have astonished a previous age. In an age of electronic communications, events in the physical world become less and less important in our perception of what is 'real' and what matters.

The media critic Marshall McLuhan said we live in a global village. If that is true, then the media is the village gossip, endlessly chattering about trivia, setting the agenda for the rest of us. Hers is the voice which nobody in the village can escape. It has been estimated that the average Briton consumes around 75 hours of media per week. Around 98 per cent of us have a TV.

Like any good gossip, the media not only recounts stories. It invents them. We recount at length the plots of last night's soaps and sitcoms. To tell what happened in the real world, slumped on a couch, occasionally shouting at the kids, is too indescribably boring to mention. The 'reality' of last night becomes a media-created virtual reality.

The 18th-century Irish philosopher George Berkeley once asked whether a tree which fell, unseen by human eye, can in any real sense be said to have fallen at all. In today's culture, many events, particularly in the realms of politics, are not considered real unless the media are watching. The journalist Simon Hoggart says we are living in 'the era of the permanent campaign',[1] where political decisions are taken less for their effectiveness or morality than for their capacity to boost somebody's chances of re-election. Image triumphs over substance and sound-bite over policy. Embodied, everyday existence ceases to be much of an end in itself. It becomes simply the raw material to be reported or filmed.

Even our warfare has become entertainment thanks to TV. During the Gulf War the bloody reality of death was sanitized into an arcade game by the computerized images of precision bombing. Zap! Pow! Gotcha!

INTO CYBERSPACE

When we grew bored with the earth, we restored our sense of wonder by looking into space. Captain Kirk, Neil Armstrong, Dr Who, Carl Sagan, Darth Vader and a host of sci-fi novelists offered to help us boldly go where no man had gone before.

However, space was not the final frontier it promised to be. To be sure, it gripped imaginations for much of the second half of the 20th century. But now space is beginning to look more like a junkyard. By 1996 the US Space Surveillance Center in the Rocky Mountains was saying there were some 8,847 objects whizzing around the earth, not to mention smaller items such as nuts and bolts from spacecraft. One estimate puts the number of fragments of human debris in orbit at 35 million. In the late '90s outer space has been increasingly replaced as the haunt of avant-garde novelists and teen fantasy by the weird and wonderful world of cyberspace.

The term was coined in the 1980s by the novelist William Gibson, to describe the extra-geographical, virtual 'universe' inside the worldwide computer network, the Internet. In this sense, cyberspace does not exist in space and time at all. It is not a location, but a vast complex of computer links crisscrossing the globe. It is a computer-generated place without any tangible reality. And yet 'real' events happen there which have a real effect in daily life. We shop there, play there, socialize there, even divorce and worship there.

To an older generation, the idea of discovering a parallel universe inside one's typewriter would have seemed bizarre in the extreme. C.S. Lewis and Lewis Carroll might have found new worlds inside wardrobes and mirrors. But Narnia and Wonderland were the stuff of children's fantasy. To Xers the Internet is becoming a real home, every bit as much as the four walls which surround them. If Baby Boomers are couch potatoes, Busters are a generation of 'mouse' potatoes, clicking their way ever deeper into the vast, unexplored wonderland of cyberspace. As more and more events 'happen' in virtual reality, our physical bodies become less and less important to us. The outside world grows less glamorous compared with the hallucinatory, unbounded universe inside our computers. The heroes and explorers of today's fiction are less likely to be the physically strong superhero than the techno-nerd, the isolated computer hacker who dares to enter the unknown territories inside his PC and emerge triumphant.

As the electronic, virtual world of the Internet bids to replace the physical world of books, paper and solid objects, the effect is to diminish our embodiment. Everyday, physical life becomes simply the pale antechamber to which we return for refuelling, the grey terminal where we rest between our flights of fantasy.

VIRTUALLY RELIGIOUS

We might think religion would help re-enchant the earth. Ironically, the ways religious experience have tended to be defined (both by outside observers and by many believers) have had the effect of further diminishing the sacredness of everyday life.

In 1912 the French sociologist Emile Durkheim published *Elementary Forms of the Religious Life*. In it he claimed all religions have one thing in common. They all classify reality into two distinct categories, 'profane' and 'sacred'. The profane is that which is familiar, routine and boring, the eating, sleeping and working which forms the backdrop to existence. The sacred, on the other hand, is an ideal dimension, set apart from the ordinary. The sacred, according to Durkheim, is a transcendent, ideal realm, above the everyday. It is the realm of awe, mystery, excitement, to be accessed in special places and through special rites. The home is profane, the church or temple is sacred. An electrician or banana-picker is profane, a clergyman or shaman is sacred. The profane pushes us deeper into our earthly life, while the sacred pulls us above it into a realm of pure spirit.

Durkheim's classifications exerted a significant influence on the study of religion. They have been the spectacles through which most analysts have viewed and categorized all religious experience. In their search for the special places, people and realms where the sacred may be found, such writers use categories which are not only alien to biblical Christianity, but also reinforce the banality of the real world. As they look at life through bifocal lenses of dualism (sacred versus profane), everything which has not been in some way sanctified is written off as 'secular' or 'ordinary'. We are denied a sense of wonder at the everyday.

If this is at odds with a biblical worldview, how have the churches fared in offering a radically alternative vision? Sadly, Christians have all too often conspired with the bifocal vision of the academics. All too often Christian believers have carved up life into categories of 'sacred' and 'secular', elevating the spiritual and despising matter, viewing human nature as a non-material soul or spirit, trapped in base matter but longing to soar to disembodied, heavenly realms. Such a picture bears little relation to the biblical view of human nature or life after death. It has more in common with the second-century heresy of Gnosticism, for which matter was irredeemably evil, a prison for pure spirit, which could only escape through esoteric knowledge and rituals.

To be an Xer is to inherit a drab, functional world of mundane and familiar objects, a world drained of wonder. But Xers have learned well the lessons taught by their culture, that excitement and awe are not found in the mundane. They are only found in escapism. Gnosticism has returned. Xers are a generation desperately looking for ways to re-enchant the earth, to see the magical in the mundane and glory in the everyday. They recognize that something vital has been lost.

RE-ENCHANTMENT

This state of affairs is an exact parallel with the late 19th century. Science, it had been thought, held all the answers. Through the advance of rational, humanistic endeavour, all humanity's problems could be solved. Religion was a fossil from a past age of ignorance and superstition.

Yet even as the death of God was being proclaimed by the thinkers, a host of other gods began to move in. Interest in the occult blossomed, and seances – in which spiritualists tried to receive messages from the spirits of the dead – became commonplace in middle-class drawing-rooms. A group of New York occultists led by the Russian-born Madame Blavatsky (real name Elena Petrovna) founded the Theosophical Society in 1875, a combination of spiritualism, Eastern mystical religion and the occult. In 1887, the Hermetic Order of the Golden Dawn was set up in London. Its founders claimed their esoteric teachings came from a group of powerful magicians, secretly working for the benefit of the world. Their goal was 'higher magic', or union with the divine, to be attained through clairvoyance, astral projection and other magical practices. The Dawn became a crucial step in the development of Western occultism.

One of the early members of the Golden Dawn was Aleister Crowley (born in 1875 to a Plymouth Brethren family), who was to become the most significant magician of the modern era, and a major influence on contemporary Satanists. Crowley adopted the title of 'The Great Beast', a description of the Antichrist in the Book of Revelation. After a row with the leadership of the Golden Dawn, Crowley travelled the world in search of occult knowledge, eventually founding what he called his new religion, based on the principle: 'Do what thou wilt shall be the whole of the Law'. His followers became notorious for their strange ceremonies, unrestrained sexuality and drug-taking.

At the same time, more mainline esoteric groups such as the Freemasons and a range of exotic Eastern religions found a new lease of life in the West, even among the apparently dry, rational leaders of Victorian society. The creator of Sherlock Holmes, Arthur Conan Doyle, devoted the latter part of his life to occultism and his attempts to photograph fairies. Sir James Frazer's book *The Golden Bough* (1890) became required reading for the educated classes, with its study of traditional and esoteric religions from around the globe, and influenced the religious thinking of a generation. The Ouija board became a commonplace of upper-class salons.

This intriguing episode in British and American life points to one overwhelming conclusion. People cannot live in a disenchanted universe. Drain away orthodox religion and our hunger for wonder and mystery is such that the old gods will return.

Generation X, raised in an age of unprecedented scientific advance and the materialistic optimism of the Thatcher and Reagan years, have been taught to build a universe on technology, progress and pragmatism. Their gurus were to be economists, advertisers and chiefs of industry. But, like their Victorian forebears, Xers have responded by looking to a very different set of gurus to re-enchant their world. Seeing in the established churches only a dry formalism, but still yearning to inhabit a sacred earth, many have embarked on a similar spiritual journey to that of the late Victorians. For many Xers the quest for the sacred remains at the level of buying Arthurian novels, CDs of Gregorian chant and posters of Celtic art. But for many, the quest for mystery and meaning is more serious. If the path of re-enchantment for the late Victorians majored on Ouija boards, spiritualism and a turn to the East, the path chosen by today's Xers is more likely to pass through the ancient traditions of their native lands.

Neo-pagans and Goddesses

The word 'pagan' stems from the Latin *paganus*, meaning 'one from the countryside' (*pagus*: a village). The neo-pagans of today trace their ancestry back to the old nature religions of pre-Christian Europe and North America. The movement includes witchcraft (also known as 'Wicca' or 'the craft'), Native American spirituality and an eclectic mix of gods and mythologies from the classical Mediterranean and the Norse and Celtic lands of Northern Europe. Most adherents exclude from their frame of reference monotheistic faiths such as Christianity, Judaism and Islam, as well as Eastern religions and Satanism. The common core to an otherwise diverse movement is a reverence for the natural world.

It is difficult to assess the scale of the current neo-pagan revival in the West. In 1989 the Occult Census of the UK estimated around 250,000 Britons could be classed as pagans or witches, with hundreds of thousands more pursuing an interest in astrology, alternative healing and psychic powers. The anthropologist David Burnett suggests a figure closer to 100,000 practising pagans, the majority of these young adults.[2] In the nominally Roman Catholic country of France, it is estimated that there are five times as many practising witches as Catholic priests. No precise figures exist for North America, but every major centre of population has a growing community which identifies with the ideals of neo-paganism. Whatever the exact numbers, it is clear that large numbers of young adults in the West are digging into their own native spiritual traditions in search of wonder and a basis for reverence towards the earth.

Neo-paganism is no single body of beliefs, but encourages a broad diversity of attitudes and practices. Most neo-pagans are suspicious of any creed, which they see as an attempt by the powerful to impose a dogma on somebody else. There are, however, certain focuses of unity. One path shared by most neo-pagans is belief in an Earth goddess.

In the ancient cultures of Greece, Rome, Northern Europe,

and among the native Americans the concept of the earth as Mother was more than just a figure of speech. Earth itself was personified as a female divinity (to the Iroquois, Eithinoha; to the Greeks, Gaia; to the Canaanites, Ashtaroth), worshipped as the sustainer of all life on earth. She was not viewed, as Christians view God, as a creator separate from the creation. Rather, she was often seen as a pantheistic goddess, immanent in nature. Advocates of the goddess cult today claim support from the British atmospheric scientist James Lovelock's 'Gaia hypothesis', published in 1979. This suggests that the astonishingly fine balance of chemical and physical conditions on the earth's surface, and in its atmosphere and oceans, points to the earth being a single, self-regulating organism, in effect a living being. Lovelock himself claims to be an agnostic in matters of religion, but others have taken his ideas as support for a reality behind the old myths of Mother Earth – an immortal, immanent life-force running through all creation.

To the neo-pagan, if the earth itself is divine, then reverence for the earth becomes a sacred duty, and a sensitivity to the natural world a religious obligation.

CRAVING WONDER

To many older people, the rediscovery of paganism and goddess-worship among young Westerners seems baffling and incomprehensible. To most Xers, however, the very bafflement of others itself seems odd. Generation X rightly recognize the anguish of living in a universe stripped of wonder, a universe from which all purpose, all presence, all the magic has been drained. The impulses behind such searching are a natural, healthy rebellion against the reductionisms of 20th-century secular humanism, which so many of us were brought up to take as axiomatic.

And yet I and many others find a fulfilment of our rebellion, our yearnings, not in neo-paganism, witchcraft or the occult, but in historic Christianity. Why did goddess worshippers in Greece and Rome turn to embrace the loving heavenly Father offered by the early Christian martyrs? How did the fresh vision of Christianity inspire the greatest Celtic artists to leave paganism and produce masterpieces such as the Book of Kells, the Lindisfarne Gospels and the intricate tracery of the Celtic crosses?

POEMS, HEROES AND MONSTERS

When I was at primary school, aged around seven or eight, I sometimes failed to turn up for lessons. Eventually, one teacher took the time to find out where I was when I should have been in class. They found me curled up with volumes of tales about the gods, goddesses and heroes of the ancient Mediterranean. Twenty-five or more years later, I still find my imagination runs riot at the mention of the names which gripped my childhood imagination: Orpheus, Zeus, Cerberus, Ariadne, Ulysses, the Cyclops.

Their world was one of adventure, heroism, tragedy, beasts, battles, passion and wonder. It was a world of poetry and fantasy. But ask that young boy whether the tales were true, and I suspect I would have said something like: 'No, of course not. They're just stories. They're not real!' I strongly suspect that if you had asked an ancient Greek or Roman, their response would not have been so different. The gods inhabited a poetic world, a world whispered into existence around fires on dark evenings. Their home was a wonderland like that dreamed up by Alice as she dozed on the banks of an Oxfordshire river. Their reality was a poetic reality, their 'truth' a poetic truth.[3]

Sometimes my small son peers down from his bunk bed and refuses to cross the darkened room in case the monsters get him. It is a fear beyond reason. Any self-respecting monster which happened to be in the room would not hesitate to slither over to his bed and scoop him out. But mythology has its secrets which reason will never grasp. The bed is a place of safety, the floor the alien territory guarded by shadow creatures. My son's monsters say more about his hungry imagination than about their hungry stomachs.

The more astute among today's neo-pagan writers readily admit much the same about their spirituality. Their return to the figures of classical mythology is not so much a way of talking about the world 'out there', as the world 'in here', in their own heads. Images such as the goddess are helpful archetypes, myths which project onto the screen of nature the structures of our own imagination. They are tales which embody the ideals which we value and by which we seek to live: femininity, love, mystery, bravery.

This makes for wonderful storytelling, but bad religion. Its bottom line is not whether beliefs are coherent and reasonable, but whether they meet a felt need in the heart of the individual. It is up to us to find a mythology which 'fits', regardless of the historical or factual basis of the myth. In reaction to the dry rationalism of the scientific West, pagans are pushing to the other extreme.

By contrast, biblical Christianity is firmly rooted in history, in the public world of observable facts. The events of the New Testament were seen by countless eye-witnesses. The books of the New Testament, the foundational documents of the faith, have been subject to more scrutiny by historians down the ages than any other ancient works. We possess more manuscripts attesting to the antiquity and authenticity of the New Testament books than for any other work from the ancient world. The Christian tradition has concurred with St Paul's insistence that the key events on which Christianity rests, such as Christ's resurrection from death, are rooted firmly in historical events. He writes to the believers in the city of Corinth, a city steeped in the myths of classical paganism:

> If there is no resurrection of the dead, then not even Christ has been raised. And if Christ has not been raised, our preaching is useless and so is your faith. More than that, we

are then found to be false witnesses about God, for we
have testified about God that he raised Christ from the dead.
(1 Corinthians 15.13–15)

Here is the astounding innovation. In Christianity, the poetic
wonder of paganism leaves the twilight world of the hearth and
enters the full sunlit glare of history. Now the magic lies not
only in our imagination, but treads the streets of first-century
Palestine.

As a child I walked the golden paths of Mount Olympus in
my imagination. As an adult I recently walked the dry earth
paths of the Mount of Olives. In the coming of Christ, something
happened of which paganism had only dreamed and told as
wild stories. Now the real earth was enchanted, the real skies
filled with angelic beings, and in a real garden a real God battled
against the real powers of Hades.

The small boy grew up to discover that the fulfilment of
paganism was not to be found in paganism. The gods, goddesses and heroes pointed beyond themselves to something
bigger and more marvellous. Like the people of the ancient
world, the boy awoke from the daydreams of wonderland, only
to find that the world about him was a real theatre of glory.

THE QUESTION OF GOODNESS

Advocates of the neo-pagan revival claim it offers a basis for the
durable values of community, trust and goodness so desperately
sought by a numbed generation. But it is easy for those in
search of ancient wisdom to have a sentimental view of ancient
paganism. Many today, particularly members of the Green
movement and some radical feminists, view paganism through
soft-focus, green-tinted glasses. They claim we need to return
to a hypothetical age of antiquity when worship of the goddess
ensured that the qualities of the feminine held sway in society
and ensured a reverence for the earth.

This vision, however, fundamentally distorts what we know

of goddesses in the ancient world. Most of them were far from the universal, benevolent mothers projected by today's neo-pagans. Many of the goddesses of the Ancient Near East – Aphrodite in Corinth, Mylitta in Babylon and Cybele in Syria – demanded temple prostitution. Many other ancient goddesses were embodiments of pure evil: the Hindu mother-deity Kali is presented as carrying a sword, a noose and a cup made from half a human skull, filled with blood; her earrings are made of dead human babies and her belt decorated with freshly severed human hands! The Ugaritic goddess Ishtar is presented in legend as a bloodthirsty psychopath. Artemis, patron deity of Ephesus, was associated with ritualized death, and human sacrifice was sometimes offered by her followers.

The goddesses and gods of ancient Greece and Rome made up a severely dysfunctional family, one which makes the worst families of today's Xers look like havens of tranquillity by comparison. Tanit of Carthage was consort to the god Baal. Both demanded the sacrifice of hundreds of live human babies. The Greek gods Zeus and Apollo repeatedly rape and then imprison or kill female mortals. There is no mystery why the ancient world turned its back on paganism. By the third century AD, 'pagan' had become a term of abuse in the Roman empire. Even ancient storytellers found themselves censuring the behaviour of their deities, the nightmare soap-opera families of antiquity. One, the Roman poet Ovid, refers to the gods' 'celestial crimes'.

In practice, the ancients tended to find their worldview for living by in the secular values of their state: allegiance to the emperor, obedience to the laws of their land. 'Religious' observance involved private devotion but was largely irrelevant to public life, except in so far as attendance at its rituals – such as sacrifice – helped ensure social conformity. The pagan gods were simply not big enough, good enough, powerful or real enough to be a basis for truth, dignity and morals. It would be like us turning to the Addams Family for a guide to spirituality and ethics.

But Xers on neo-pagan paths ignore the historical reality of paganism, preferring a sanitized, Athena-card version, custom-recycled for environmentally aware, spiritually starved post-moderns. Sentimentalized representations of pagan life gloss over harsh truths of history. For every benevolent Gaia there was a bloody Artemis or Ishtar. The Iroquois Five Nations tribe of Native Americans, who worshipped the earth goddess Eithinoha – Our Mother – also massacred their neighbours the Huron. The Iroquois Six Nations killed off the Iroquois Family tribe.

Christians believe we inhabit a moral universe, where our concepts of good and evil exist because they are rooted in the character of the Creator himself. For the Christian, the ultimate value is self-sacrificing love, following the example of Christ. The God who cares for widows, orphans and outsiders, and the Christ who gives himself for others are our role-models. True power for the Christian can only be relational and sacrificial.

On the other hand the American witch Starhawk, one of the leaders of the Wiccan revival and a bestselling author, writes that the goal of Wicca is about 'personal power. We all strive to increase our power-from-within.'[4] The way to increase this personal, inner power is through magic. All gods, myths, landscapes, rituals and relationships are a means of inner, personal empowering. There is little basis for compassion built into the system. It begins to look more like a green and sanctified selfishness.

A pagan might reply that this is to misunderstand their faith, that paganism is essentially relational, since in a pantheistic system we are all inseparably bound together. Books about the goddess are filled with claims that since she is the life-force of the whole earth, we all participate in that life. Pagans criticize the Christian God, whom they (wrongly) stereotype as masculine, remote, warlike and indifferent, as offering little basis for an ethic of global harmony.

In fact, for all its noble ideals, the pantheism of neo-paganism actually undermines personal dignity. If earth, sky, sea, animals, plants and humans are merely dimensions of a universal goddess, all that ultimately matters is the grand whole. No part of that whole can claim to have more significance than any other. We only have a role insofar as we use ritual to immerse ourselves in the broad flow of life. None of us is of fundamental importance or value in ourselves. We function only as blurred parts of a bigger pattern, a pattern which is beyond our imposed categories of right and wrong.

The pagan answer to our quest for personal values is to reply that we have no personal value. Its advice to a generation longing to erase selfishness is to erase the self. Contemporary witches are correct to say Wicca does not have a concept of good and evil.[5] Sin becomes a meaningless concept if the ultimate reality is the goddess, who embodies in herself all light and dark, right and wrong, truth and falsehood. Certainly, there can be no question of the Christian insistence of a primal distortion in human nature known as sin.

WONDER REDISCOVERED

Xers are a generation in search of older gods, gods who will repair the damage done to the earth in the name of our cultural idols of individualism, materialism and technology. The Christian claim is that these dreams and aspirations are met in the God of the Bible, a God who entered history in the person of Jesus of Nazareth.

Christianity asserts that creation is a gift, a visible reminder of the Creator, and that humans are called to be God's caring stewards of the earth. It has been said that the crisis of the atheist is when he feels overwhelmed by the sheer gift of life, but has nobody to thank. This sense of gratitude before the gifts of God in creation is fundamental to many of the Psalms in the Bible. The Psalmist shares an affinity with the beauty of creation just as much as any pagan or nature-mystic, but departs from paganism when he recognizes it all as the handiwork of a loving, personal Creator. In Psalm 148, the imagery of nature tumbles over itself in grateful torrents:

Praise the LORD from the earth,
you great sea creatures and all ocean depths,
lightning and hail, snow and clouds,
stormy winds that do his bidding,
you mountains and all hills,
fruit trees and all cedars,
wild animals and all cattle,
small creatures and flying birds,
kings of the earth and all nations,
you princes and all rulers on earth,
young men and maidens,
old men and children.' (Psalm 148.7–12)

The poet moves beyond paganism in his gratitude that the gift has a personal giver:

Let them praise the name of the LORD,
for he commanded and they were created.
He set them in place for ever and ever;
he gave a decree that will never pass away. (Psalm 148.5, 6)

GOD'S CLOTHING

However, in the perspective of historic Christianity, the earth is not only a gift from God. It actually offers a glimpse into the life of God himself. The Psalms make explicit something implied throughout Scripture: the creation is an extension of the Creator, his 'clothing':

O LORD my God, you are very great;
you are clothed with splendour and majesty.
He wraps himself in light as with a garment. (Psalm 104.1, 2)

He made darkness his covering, his canopy around him –
the dark rain clouds of the sky. (Psalm 18.11)

God in himself might be invisible to the human eye, but the 'splendour and majesty' which clothe him are the evidence of his presence. Like royalty, God is robed in splendour, but God's robe is his creation, the natural world.

God is present in the skies, wind, fire, and storms. Creation is charged up with his 'glory', the visible majesty which radiates from him. The Hebrews called it the *shekinah*, the glory which shines from God as the evidence of his presence on earth. The seraphs who address Isaiah remind him that the *shekinah* of the Creator is not a remote, distant force, but fills the globe. Every twig and branch, cloud and star point beyond themselves to a personal presence:

Holy, holy, holy is the LORD Almighty;
the whole earth is full of his glory. (Isaiah 6.3).

There is another way, however, in which the Christian understanding of nature differs from that of the secular humanists and the neo-pagans, on an issue of vital concern to Generation X. It is the question of how we react to the evil and brokenness in our world. Both secularists and pagans assume, in their different ways, that the world cannot be fundamentally different from the way it is at present. The secularists, because they see only a closed system of cause and effect and natural laws; the pagans, because they see people simply as part of the cosmic life-force, able to experience their interconnectedness, but unable to stand aside and question it. Paganism has to account for the evident evil and wrong in the system with tales of mischievous gods and goddesses, or else by claiming that a universal god or goddess embodies in their own person not only good, but also evil. Neither option gives a reassuring basis for human moral action, or for believing that evil has an antidote.

Christianity, however, insists that the present state of our world is not fully the way it was meant to be. Evil is a reality, both in the natural world and in the human heart. For the Christian, there is space to collaborate with the redemptive purposes of a God, in whom there is no darkness at all, in bringing healing to creation.

STEWARDS OF THE EARTH

As we interact with the created world, we not only encounter the wonder of the earth, we also find the roots of our own identity. We discover our full humanity as stewards of the earth, acting as its responsible caretakers. Ours is the task of a trusted intermediary, representing creation to God, and God to creation.

An announcement of this commission is given in Genesis: 'The LORD God took the man [*Adam*: humanity] and put him in the Garden of Eden to work it and take care of it' (Genesis 2.15). In the Genesis account, stewardship over the earth has two dimensions: working it and caring for it. The Christian has a God-given mandate for ecology. The Hebrew word used for caring, *samar*, means to watch, protect, tend and keep from harm. Christians should be in the forefront of environmental concern, because their motivation to tend the planet and keep it safe is a primary calling from God.

This is no mandate for some back-to-nature pastoral idyll. The other word used, *abad*, means to work the earth, to serve it, to use it creatively. It is a reminder that the human task is to take the raw material of creation and develop it creatively as described in Genesis 1.26–30. In this 'cultural mandate', to which we referred in Chapter 1, the Bible tells us that it is our calling to find satisfaction and identity in all our culture-forming tasks – arts, science and business just as much as in agriculture and botany.

CREATION RENEWED

The pagan vision is of the universal harmony of all nature on an innocent earth. It is a fine dream, inspiring cultures of great art and literature: from the ancient world, the classical revivalists of Renaissance Europe, and among modern-day pagan idealists.

But where does the dream come from? And how is it to be attained? It is in reality Christianity alone which claims that our dreams of Eden are a nostalgia for a real place, for a lost innocence. Christianity alone claims that the earth will one day be renewed, that a day will come when all the highest dreams of paganism become a reality. It is a vision elaborated in the Book of Revelation (see in particular Revelation 21), and foreseen by the Hebrew prophets (for example, in Isaiah 60). It is a vision of a day when the lion and lamb shall lie together, swords will be beaten into ploughshares, and all nations, genders and races of the earth will live together in harmony.

For now, in the interim period of history, the Christian knows that as stewards we are called to be the creative caretakers of a world which is flawed, but nonetheless still charged up with the glory of its Creator. We are also to be those who are 'looking for the city that is to come' (Hebrews 13.14), signposts to the final fulfilment of the dreams of the ages, a Day when the earth will be filled with the innocent wonder of a fresh new morning, and the old order of things will have passed away.

CHAPTER SIX

GOD:
THE WONDER OF
ENCOUNTER

But then I must remind myself we are living creatures – we
have religious impulses – we *must* – and yet into what
cracks do these impulses flow in a world without religion?
It is something I think about every day. Sometimes I think it
is the only thing I should be thinking about.

Douglas Coupland, *Life After God*

THE REVENGE OF GOD

One could almost feel sorry for the secular humanists: Karl Marx,
Bertrand Russell, Julian Huxley, A.J. Ayer, Richard Dawkins, *et al*.
For so long things seemed to be going their way. But then, just
as final victory seemed certain and the last rumours of gods,
angels and demons appeared to have been killed off, back they
all come with renewed vigour. God is having the last laugh. Of
all the endangered species on the earth today, *homo secularus*
looks least likely to survive.

Quite a reversal from the picture of religion in the modern
world which held sway from the 19th century to as recently
as the 1970s. Victorian thinkers such as Herbert Spencer and
Thomas Huxley wrenched the theory of evolution from biology,
applied it to society, and renamed it 'progress'. Just as animal
species which survive were considered fitter and better adapted

to their conditions, so too the newer forms of society – scientific, rational and industrial – were held to be superior. Religion was a feature of pre-industrial, primitive cultures, the product of a worldview which was no longer tenable.

It is sobering to realize that, for all its sound and fury, secularism was the brief aberration in history. Despite all the best efforts of the atheists, the children they spawned are returning to religion in droves. Or perhaps the rebellion into God has been *because* of the very secularism of their parents. They have seen the products of 'progress' and 'enlightenment', and do not like what they see.

Around the globe, religious faith is resurgent. Fundamentalist Islam grips the hearts of idealistic young Arabs. Across the USA, 'megachurches' of over 2,000 members flourish in most towns and cities. Fully 40 per cent of all Americans are in church on any given Sunday, and a range of alternative religious options are busy crowding into the Western marketplace. Indigenous traditions such as paganism, Native American spirituality and shamanism are being rediscovered. New Age stores sell tarot cards, model pyramids, healing crystals and the I-Ching. And angels are making a comeback, with large sections of bookstores and even whole shops devoted to the sale of angel books, pictures, models, hangings and ornaments.

RELATIVELY TRUE

However, for most people in the West the return to faith is no simple return to pre-secularism. For all the resurgence of interest in the spiritual, the official figures for church attendance continue to slide, particularly in Europe. The Church of England's 1996 report, *Youth A Part*, revealed that church attendance of 14- to 21-year-olds dropped by over a third in the seven years between 1987 and 1994. The USA too is seeing a slow decline in overall church attendance, with the slide of the mainline denominations (such as Methodists, Episcopalians and Presbyterians) being particularly steep.

In an earlier chapter we suggested that Western history can be divided into three big eras: the premodern, the modern and the postmodern. In religious terms, if premodernity was the era dominated by a single religion – Christianity, modernity was dominated by a single dogma – secular progress. What then of postmodernity? The postmodern world is dominated by a single impulse – *personal choice*.

If a medieval peasant had been asked what, for her, was the bottom line of religion, she might have said the following: 'The fact that God exists, and can be known through the Church.' If a Victorian secularist had been asked the same question, he might have said: 'The fact that God doesn't exist, because we have no scientific proof that he does.'

But ask the same question to a Generation Xer, raised in a climate of postmodernity, and he is more likely to say: 'It's up to everybody to find whatever is true for them.' The postmodern world is deeply suspicious of any claims to absolute truths, including the truths of secularism. All '-isms' are suspect. Marxism is discredited. Many of the older, established churches are slowly emptying. No single vision commands such wide-spread support as relativism, the view that there are no absolutes binding on everybody.

It must be over a decade since anybody said to me, 'You're a Christian – give me some proof that God actually exists.' On the other hand, scarcely a month goes by without a young person asking why Christians feel the need to convince anybody else that their faith is true, or telling me with dogmatic certainty that 'all religions are the same'. I remember one student staring at me in utter disbelief when I claimed that Christianity might be true in a way that other systems were not. She could hardly understand what I was saying: 'So you're saying it's true for you. But if somebody else finds something different which is just as true for them, then how can you say your way is better? And anyway, all the religions are saying the same things, aren't they?'

There has been a sea-change in the popular consciousness

over the past two decades or so. We have moved from the assumption that if something is true, then by definition a contradictory view must be untrue; that somewhere, out there, is a single 'big picture' which is true for everybody, and which religion and philosophy have to discover. We have moved to a belief that nobody has a monopoly on truth, that there is probably no single 'big story' to be found. The best we can do is find something which works for us and makes us happy.

The way this is expressed in religious terms is that 'ultimate reality' is an unknowable mystery, which we each need to encounter in our own way. The Californian author Matthew Fox is typical of the postmodern mindset when he likens the religious quest to the attempt to draw water from a deep, underground river. The representatives of all religions and philosophies sit around their wells, each lowering buckets. Each might believe theirs is the only true well, but all ultimately descend to the river which is God, who is beyond all definitions and all systems.

This model of religious 'truth' has an enormous appeal for Xers, whose dominant value is relational. In this view that all religions are equally valid, all truth relative, and all that matters is whether it works for you, Xers believe they have found a key to greater global harmony and tolerance. So where has this new relativist consensus come from?

BORN TO SHOP

Most people for most of human history have lived in cultures of subsistence, in societies where people work to stay alive. Workers provide for the immediate needs of their own families and villages. Food is grown locally, clothes are made by local people. The one exception to this might be royalty and nobility, those with the wealth to have others consistently farming, manufacturing and producing luxury goods for them.

In the West, from the late 19th century on, this pattern changed decisively. For the first time, techniques of mass production and faster means of transportation, such as the railways, meant more goods could be produced than were needed for personal survival. The kind of luxuries restricted to the ruling classes started to become a possibility for people at all levels of society. Brand names, in existence since the early 19th century but little used, became a popular way for manufacturers to encourage loyal purchasing of their own products.

Europeans and Americans, weary of the privations caused by the Second World War, eagerly joined in the consumer boom of the 1950s and '60s. Back in the mid-19th century the English economist and philosopher John Stuart Mill had defined true freedom as 'pursuing our own good in our own way, so long as we do not attempt to deprive others of theirs, or impede their efforts to attain it'. In other words, freedom is freedom of personal choice. All that ultimately matters is that the free individual has the right to make his own decisions. Everything else – society, obligations to others, the common good – is secondary.

With the arrival of post-war consumerism, Mill's definition of freedom has walked off the page and into the shopping precinct. Here, at last, is the ultimate embodiment of personal liberty. I can define my very identity by the consumer choices I make. I go to the stores I choose, to buy the foods, the training shoes, the jackets, the furniture which best expresses my chosen 'lifestyle'. And while I make my self-defining choices, others are free to do the same.

The supermarket shelf has also become the model for how we shop for truth and meaning. All that matters is choice, and older, more absolute criteria of truth become obsolete. The man next to me in the canned fruit aisle might choose prunes. I choose guavas. He chooses Sikhism. I choose Christianity.[1]

For the postmodern consumer of faiths, the act of choosing is actually more important than what we each choose. Religion, like prunes and guavas, is a lifestyle choice, where rules give way to preferences. I choose therefore I am.

FROM MASS TO MASS MEDIA

Television has become much more than something we look at.
It has become a way of looking, the window through which we
watch the world. Normally, we expect to look through a window
and see a clear image of whatever lies behind it. However, a
window whose glass is tinted or distorted will affect the colour
or the shape of the reality we see. So it is with TV. In a culture
dominated by mass media, we take the watching eye of TV for
granted. We no longer ask ourselves whether our ways of looking might have an inherent bias or flaw.

But TV unquestionably has a bias. It relativizes all claims to
truth. On TV the whole world is brought into our living room,
including the world of religion. In the past few months I have
seen programmes on British TV about Buddhist corpse collectors
in Bangkok, a Haitian voodoo priestess living in Brooklyn, Islamic
revivalists, new avenues in Christian worship and New Agers
learning sexual technique in suburban London.

Each is presented in the same dispassionate, intrigued tone.
No criteria of truth or value are brought to bear. No comparison
is made between rival truth claims. Even those views which are
patently ridiculous are presented with apparent seriousness: the
man who has sat in his armchair for the past ten years watching
TV, defending his slobbishness; the man who leaves his
Christmas decorations up all year round because he loves the
festive season so much. People who claim to have seen post-
death appearances of Elvis are presented alongside Christians
who claim to have met with the risen Christ.

The medium not only conveys the message: it becomes the
message. An intrinsically relativizing medium promotes the
message that all truth is relative. Our media is rich in information, but poor at enabling critical discernment. Any face-to-face
meeting with somebody who claims to have found religious
truth is met with a weary shrug of the shoulders: 'I saw a man
the other evening who said he was God. And last week I
watched a woman who said God told her to kill her husband.

And I've seen all those fanatics shouting in the streets in Iran. So what? We all find our own truth in our own way.'

JUNG, NIETZSCHE, FEUERBACH

One of the thinkers who has given intellectual credibility to the idea that all religious truth is relative is the psychologist Carl Gustav Jung (1875–1961), son of a Swiss Reformed clergyman. One of the key claims of Jung is that each individual has not only a personal unconscious mind, but that there is such a thing as a collective unconscious, built up through history and shared by all humanity.

We tend to think of each person as individuals, formed by their own culture, background and commitments. Each person's mind is seen as separate from other minds: full of its own thoughts, preferences and values. But Jung claims that beneath the superficial differences are universal patterns or structures, common to all human minds, which form the basis of our thinking and self-understanding. We are not aware of these deeper strata in normal, conscious life, but patterns or archetypes surface when the rational mind is not in control, particularly through dreams, mythologies and fantasies. Jung immersed himself in the study of ancient myths, claiming that the figures and tales found there embody not just archaic but universal motifs of human consciousness.

Archetypes stalking our unconscious minds include the *anima*, or female archetype, the *animus*, or male archetype, the child, the earth mother and the hero. Wholeness, or 'individuation', comes from forging a healthy link between the conscious mind and the personal and collective unconscious, from accepting and respecting those hidden parts of our mind which surface in myth and dream. According to Jung, this journey to psychological wholeness can best be achieved with the help of an analyst.

Talk of gods and goddesses is for Jung a way of talking about ourselves. He claims all people have 'a natural religious condition', and our psychological health depends on being in touch with this part of our own make-up. Archetypes of gods and archetypes of one's own self become indistinguishable. Any idea of a transcendent, personal being beyond the self is dismissed by Jung, a lifelong occultist. The real task is to honour our inner archetypes in the search for personal wholeness, to discover the god within.

For the militantly anti-Christian German philosopher Friedrich Nietzsche (1844–1900), all religion was simply a power play of one person or group against another. For him, any talk of 'truth' and a claim to have access to universal or objective reality was no more than a disguise for personal advantage. All people possess an innate 'will to power', to dominate others, and religion offers ample opportunities. Similarly, he claimed that morality was based on no more than a desire to preserve order in society. It too is all about power games. Since Nietzsche (coincidentally, also the son of a clergyman, in the Lutheran Church), it can no longer be assumed that God is 'out there', that religious people are devout seekers after truth, and their morality simple obedience to the ways of God.

A third thinker whose name is less well known, but whose views have had a profound influence through the works of Marx, Engels, Huxley, Freud and the novelist George Eliot, was Ludwig Feuerbach (1804–72). It was Feuerbach, and not Marx, who first described religion as opium. An explicitly anti-Christian thinker, like Nietzsche, Feuerbach's big idea was that our talk about God was actually talk about ourselves. God was 'merely the projected essence of man'.

Human beings, according to this theory, have a range of natural ideals, fears and aspirations. These are then projected outside ourselves and given the shapes of deities and heroes. The Christian God, for Feuerbach, was a personification of our own feelings of contentment and security. Religion was not a window into the beyond, but a mirror in which people could see their own reflections.

Taken together, the effects of the mass media, the consumer

society and the legacy of Jung, Nietzsche and Feuerbach have had a powerful effect on the way young adults in our culture think about questions of truth in religion. Even if people have not heard the names of these thinkers, or ever examined the social shifts of postmodernity, they will have inhaled such perspectives simply by living in their culture. They will almost certainly have been taught relativism in beliefs and morals as a self-evident truth in school and college. In the name of equality and tolerance – both in themselves excellent virtues – students have been led to believe that the only safe route toward these goals is the absolute openness of relativism. Reality becomes the reality you choose or create for yourself. No version of truth or goodness can claim a universal allegiance.

Most will rarely question that religion is a quest for inner wholeness, that truth is relative, that what is right for you might not be right for me. Heresy lies not in untruth, but intolerance.

SPIRITUALITY

How, then, can we account for the revival of interest in religion amongst today's young adults, if their belief in – and concern for – truth has collapsed? The answer can be given in one word: spirituality.

Spirituality is on sale at a High Street and shopping centre near you. Spirituality is fashion accessories, toiletries, wall-hangings, CDs and perfumes. A fashion spread in a recent women's style magazine hailed a return to 'spirituality' through the use of natural, undyed fabrics. Toiletries not tested on animals are advertised as embodying 'spiritual' values. Gifts made from recycled materials are billed as expressing the 'spiritual' side of our nature. Jenny, 21, was typical of her generation when she told me: 'I never go to church myself, but I'm really into spirituality.'

But what does it all mean? What is 'spirituality' as defined by the the gurus of the magazine and shopping mall? One of the few places I have found an attempt at a definition is in a leaflet advertising aromatherapy oils. The London-based Aroma-therapy Associates have a leaflet explaining the philosophy behind their products. They describe their oils as being for 'the treatment of the whole person', and their different oils are 'grouped according to their effect on Body, Mind or Spirit'. But what is Spirit? The leaflet continues: 'We use the term "Spirit" to convey our innermost self – the more subtle side of our nature which cannot always express itself in the turmoil of our emotions', and suggests that the oils will be beneficial in 'help-ing to achieve a sense of balance and composure'.

Spirituality, then, means some capacity in each individual for personal depth, something akin to our emotions, but more timeless and ethereal. It is our capacity for creativity, and a deep inner sense of equilibrium and wellbeing. It might be evoked by a CD of Gregorian chant. It might equally be aroused by shop-ping in an ethnic rug shop, by watching a TV programme about the Amazon, or recycling household waste.

Anything can be a resource in the personal development of 'spirituality', so long as it appears to foster inner depth and a sense of mystery. Whenever I go to a religious retreat house, I like to ask other visitors their reason for being there. The most frequent answer is: 'To deepen my personal spirituality.'

It is interesting to see that this definition of spirituality is even becoming common within Christian churches. I recently attended a study day run by the organizers of one of the UK's leading Christian festivals. One of the optional workshops was on the theme of spirituality, where we were each given a sheet, containing a number of definitions of spirituality, and asked to underline the one we felt best embodied its meaning. I underlined one which said something to the effect of 'Being empowered by the Spirit of God to live a Christian life in today's world'.

The other members of the group, all of whom described themselves as Christians, opted for definitions such as: 'A deep, inner feeling in myself', 'My inner impulse for reaching to God', or 'A mystical sense of inner harmony', or 'My profound sense of the mystery in nature'. Some of them ridiculed my choice for omitting words such as 'inner', 'deep', 'natural', and 'mystical', which they associated with the concept of spirituality.

A close look at how the term 'spirituality' is being used today, particularly by Xers, is instructive. It shows that spirituality is a capacity located wholly in the self. For the Xer, it is simply taken for granted that spirituality is a type of self-realization and self-expression. It is almost a synonym for 'the inner life'. We see 'spirituality' in action in the work of Thomas Moore, one of today's most popular spiritual gurus, whose work is characteristic of much recent spiritual writing.

THOMAS MOORE

Care of the Soul (subtitled A Guide for Cultivating Depth and Sacredness in Everyday Life)[2] by Thomas Moore spent over 46 weeks on the *New York Times* bestseller list, following its publication in 1992, and has become one of America's top selling books of spiritual guidance.

Moore is a former Roman Catholic monk who now writes and lectures on Jungian psychology. Moore's key to 'cultivating depth and sacredness in everyday life' lies in the rediscovery of what he calls 'soul'. He admits that he cannot define what 'soul' actually is, but through the book he offers a few clues. It is 'to do with genuineness and depth' (xi), it is 'a quality or a dimension of experiencing life and ourselves' (5), the 'infinite depth of a person and of a society, comprising all the many mysterious aspects that go together to make up our identity', and it is 'the mystery we glimpse when we look deeply into ourselves' (267). At one point, Moore gives up on definitions, claiming, 'When we say that someone or something has soul, we know what we mean, but it is difficult to specify exactly what that meaning is' (5). He makes some intriguing assumptions, since he also tells us, 'You have a soul, the tree in front of your house has a soul, but so too does the car parked under that tree' (268).

115

Moore seems to be saying that soul is a capacity which each of us has for being deep, for going beyond the superficial and seeing a mysterious dimension in all things. Terms such as 'deep' and 'depth' appear on almost every page. In other words, Moore means by 'soul' what most people mean by 'spirituality'. He notes that traditionally the clergy were charged with the 'cure' or 'care' of souls. Now, he says, 'we can be the curates of our own souls, an idea that implies an inner priesthood and a personal religion' (xv). It is up to each of us to develop our own spirituality.

We can each do this in a variety of ways. One is by creating our own places of sacredness: boxes of memories, albums of photos, or personal journals (215). But the main ways we care for our soul (and, presumably, that of our car) are by studying our own dreams, and by immersing ourselves in myths, rituals and religious traditions of every kind. Dreams are important because they form 'a person's own mythology and imagery' (217), offering insights into the working of our unconscious minds.

Here the influence of Jung is clear. For Moore, all religions and all mythologies are mirrors into our own unconscious. They reveal the 'archetypes' inside our own brains, inherited jointly by all humanity from primitive times. Religion and ritual do not offer a window into a reality beyond the self, but help the self understand its own inner workings. For example, Moore follows Jung in claiming that one of our inner archetypes is the *puer* (Latin for 'boy') or the idealistic, energetic, boyish impulse. He claims the best places to find the *puer* embodied are in Jesus (who calls himself 'Son', is at odds with the establishment, and so on), and also in the person of Gautama Buddha and in Shakespeare's Hamlet (250). Jesus standing in the Jordan to be baptized by John is actually an archetype for each of us of wanting to live life to the full, to 'step courageously into the river of existence, instead of finding ways to remain safe, dry and unaffected' (244). And the passion of Jesus is actually an archetype of the story of love, along with the stories of Odysseus, Hamlet, and Tristan and Isolde (82).

The picture-language of Christian tradition is no more significant than any other. We can equally turn to Zen, classical Greek myths, medieval occultists, Arthurian romances, Plato and our own dreams in the search for depth. We read the Bible not to find the self-revelation of God, but as a stimulus to our own 'religious imagination' (239). Moore claims that one day we will move beyond all the truth-claims of the different religions, and see all religion, ritual and mythology for what they really are: a resource for our own self-analysis. Myths and religions are our decorated mirrors: gilded, beautiful, but ultimately only showing us ourselves: 'One day I expect an "archetypal theology" may show us the soul of religious texts from around the world' (239). What the soul needs, says Moore, is more myths, more dreams, more religion.

DEEP WITHIN

Moore is typical of a newer generation of writers on spiritual themes who are helping shape the religious consciousness of a generation. In reaction against what they see as the superficiality of contemporary culture, they stress the need for depth, for cultivating the inner life and a sense of the spiritual.

It is an appealing vision to a generation turned onto the inner life and the sphere of the spirit, but turned off by formal religious structures. 'Spirituality' appears to offer Xers the most appealing features of religion, but without what they see as its worst features. It offers inner tranquillity, a myth to live by and a sense of mystery, but without exclusive claims to truth and morality. It enables me to go deeper in my own journey of self-realization, but without treading on the toes of anybody else.

But is contemporary spirituality built on a solid foundation, and does it have the capacity to change people and societies for the better?

PILLSBURY DOUGHBOY SPIRITUALITY

When I was younger my favourite TV commercial featured the Pillsbury Doughboy, a small, roly-poly figure made of bread dough. His white, doughy face beamed benevolently from the TV screen and broadened into a chuckle when a finger poked his ample stomach.

Sometimes I like to imagine a group of spiritually hungry bakers getting together to design their own religion. What, they ask, will be an authentic spirituality for breadmakers? They decide to set up small altars in their shops and homes and pay homage to the Pillsbury Doughboy. What could be more appropriate than a god who not only affirms breadmaking, but who actually is bread himself? If Doughboy is the central deity in the bakers' pantheon, then a range of other minor gods also help: Jesus Christ (who broke bread, told his followers that he was 'the bread of life', and made references to yeast); and the great Mr Kipling, who reminds us that in all our activities we must be exceedingly good. They develop a site of pilgrimage: the steep cobbled street in the Hovis advertisements. They find an array of references to breadmaking in all the myths and faiths of the world, which they put together as their scriptures under the title: *Daily Bread*.

Always they are motivated by a single guiding principle: what I as a baker think will suit me, what will bring me fulfilment in my breadmaking way of life.

SPIRITUALITY AND TRUTH

But why would most of us find Doughboy religion half-baked? Surely because fictional bakers can only sustain their Doughboy religion by doing away with any criterion of truth and untruth. They have redefined truth to mean simply whatever suits them and their lifestyle. Just as inside their own heads, everything is bread, so in the realm of the spirit everything becomes bread.

True wonder, an encounter with that which is other than the self, is excluded from the recipe.

Now instead of bakers, let us imagine the children of the post-war consumer boom in search of religion. They are a culture raised on an unparalleled choice of foods from around the world, an unprecedented range of media options, a vast choice of clothing, furnishings, reading-matter and leisure pursuits. For such people the one non-negotiable is that they stand at the centre of their own universe, able to select the goods, people and experiences they choose. Such a culture goes off in search of religion and comes up with 'spirituality', their very own version of Doughboy religion. It is a religion where the self is at the centre, where all the faiths and myths of history are trawled in the search for happy inner experiences, where nobody and nothing impedes freedom of choice. It is spirituality as lifestyle accessory.

The spirituality of Thomas Moore and other such writers is not a genuine spirituality of wonder and astonishment. It is a Doughboy spirituality for a self-centred consumer society. For a generation reared on endless Saturdays standing in front of shop mirrors, trying on the latest style of jeans, Moore's definition of truth may be curiously comforting: 'Soul knows the relativity of its claim on truth. It is always in front of a mirror, always in speculative mode, watching itself discover its developing truth, knowing that subjectivity and imagination are always in play' (246). All we can ever really know is the experience of trying on and buying whatever appears to fit comfortably.

SPIRITUALITY AND GOODNESS

Contemporary spirituality not only assumes that all truth is relative. It is also happy to believe that morals are relative too: we create our own standards of right and wrong. For Moore, soul has its own laws, unbounded by convention and traditional ethics. Any other approach is guilty of being 'moralistic' (85).

So he is happy to claim that soul is 'a form of consciousness with its own wisdom' (86), that whatever wild imaginings lurk inside us are to be welcomed and celebrated: 'Care of the soul means respecting its emotions and fantasies, however objectionable' (85). The only law is that we must follow the dictates of love, wherever it leads, and especially if it leads beyond the confines of orthodox morality: 'every love involves a transgression. Soul is to be found in the vicinity of taboo' (85).

This fundamentally self-centred ethic is seen most clearly in Moore's attitudes towards intimate relationship with another person, particularly in sexuality. In earlier chapters we considered such intimacy as an encounter with one who is other than ourselves, that the heart of love is encounter and respect. This understanding is explicitly denied by Moore:

> It may be useful to consider love less as an aspect of relationship and more an event of the soul. This is the point of view taken in ancient handbooks. There is no talk of making relationships work . . . The emphasis is on what love does to the soul. (78)

And if this is true, it naturally follows that love is whatever appears to bring me personal fulfilment. It should come as no surprise to learn that eight years after Jung married his wife, Emma Rauschenbach, he also took a mistress, Antonia Wolff, a relationship which lasted until his death. Although the triangular arrangement was difficult for both women, Jung was being consistent. All that ultimately mattered was his own, self-defined happiness and 'wholeness'.

CARING FOR THE SOUL OF GENERATION X

Any Xer with her wits about her cannot fail to spot the tragic irony.

Generation X has inherited a world ravaged by an ideology which claims that humankind is the measure of all things. Rainforests are felled, countryside destroyed, seas polluted, and poorer nations kept in poverty by a system based on personal comfort and consumer choice in the affluent West. They are a generation which has felt all too acutely the destructive power of divorce run riot, a generation emotionally numbed and fearful of walking the streets at night. They long for a wonder which constantly eludes them. The toll of damage seen by Xers in their own lives and in the world is the direct consequence of rampant relativism in truth and morals.

Then their spiritual gurus suggest that the solution lies in fostering a spirituality of selfish individualism. But for all the use of vogue terms such as 'deep', 'profound', 'inner' and 'mystery', such a spirituality is appallingly shallow. Not only does it fail to challenge the complacency of Western consumer capitalism, it is a product of it. Not only does it fail to challenge personal selfishness, it is its religious expression.

Such is the religious illiteracy of our culture that we fail to spot that such 'spirituality' is no solution. We live in an age which can tell the difference between Coke and Pepsi, but not between good religion and bad religion. Consumer spirituality, far from being the answer, is simply a restatement of the problem using mystical jargon.

THEOLOGY AND ME-OLOGY

If theology is the study of God (from the Greek *theos*), then most contemporary spirituality is 'me-ology', the art of taking my own tastes, preferences and moods and creating a customized religion just for me.

For all their talk of transcendence, eternity, the spirit and sacredness, spiritual writers such as Moore say nothing about God. From the perspective of historic Christianity, this is an alarming omission. It means that the one central Reality which can give us bearings in the search for spirituality, identity and wonder is being left out of the picture. We are left with what the theologian David Wells calls the 'weightlessness of God'. [3]

Instead of being opened to the Mind behind the universe,

you are left shut up inside the universe of your own mind. The gods of the new spirituality can inspire no wonder. They are as controllable and safe as the Doughboy, a projection of our own consumer preferences. In his classic, *Miracles*, C.S. Lewis expresses well the tremor which passes down the human spine at the suspicion that perhaps God might be real, that he might be more than mere projection:

> There comes a moment when the children who have been playing at burglars hush suddenly: was that a *real* footstep in the hall? There comes a moment when people who have been dabbling in religion ('Man's search for God'!) suddenly draw back. Supposing we really found Him? We never meant it to come to *that*!'[4]

Lewis underlines the vital Christian insight that there is such a thing as truth, but that this truth is a Person. The discovery of truth comes neither from navel-gazing nor abstract contemplation. It forces us outwards, into an encounter with One other than ourselves. Moses is confronted with a burning bush, Saul is thrown from his horse and blinded, Isaiah collapses in a gibbering heap, crying 'Woe to me!' The biblical meeting with God is no comfortable spirituality. It is a terrifying and awe-inspiring encounter.

In Acts 2 we read of the disciples of Jesus, together in an upper room:

> Suddenly a sound like the blowing of a violent wind came from heaven and filled the whole house where they were sitting. They saw what seemed to be tongues of fire that separated and came to rest on each of them. All of them were filled with the Holy Spirit . . . (Acts 2.2–4)

As Peter and the others dash downstairs to shout out to the world what has just happened, I sometimes picture a distant ancestor of Jung remaining upstairs and speculating on which archetype had just surfaced from the collective unconscious. But this was no archetype. It was people experiencing the raw, unleashed power of a personal God, a God beyond all their petty projections, preferences and pieties.

On the day of Pentecost, we see the true basis for Christian Spirituality, the intimate presence of the third person of the Trinity. The Christian response to spirituality (with a small 's') is Spirituality (with a capital 'S'), life charged up with the personal Spirit of God and lived out in the world.

The true God can never be tamed and domesticated. In the words of the novelist Annie Dillard:

> Does anyone have the foggiest idea what sort of power we so blithely evoke? Or, as I suspect, does no one believe a word of it? . . . It is madness to wear ladies' straw hats and velvet hats to church; we should all be wearing crash helmets. Ushers should issue life preservers and signal flares; they should lash us to our pews.[5]

When Christians await Sunday morning with bated breath and trembling with excitement, filled with awe and wonder at coming into the presence of a living God, then perhaps the watching world will stop playing at spirituality and join us.

IDENTITY

Today's free-for-all 'spirituality' might feel like a victory over older, dogmatic images of God. It might feel like a liberation from the creeds and definitions which plagued theologians of earlier centuries. It soon becomes clear, however, that our victory is hollow and brief. Liberation from the 'constraints' of God means liberation from the roots of human identity.

To be made in the image of God is to be made for relationship with him. God is no projection of our own ideals, values or preferences. We are not made to be alone, or to find our ultimate reference point in ourselves. Over against all the inner diggings of 'spirituality', Christianity insists that we can only discover truth by looking beyond ourselves to God himself, the God who is really there and who is Other. God made us for an encounter, for intimacy with himself. The Hebrew words for worship, *hishahawah* and *abodah*, mean 'bowing before' God, and 'serving' him with our lives. Worship opens us outwards. It is an antidote to self-centredness.

This is why the Old Testament prophets denounce the worship of idols. It is not that in making substitute gods the people of Israel were breaking some arbitrary law, but that they were being unfaithful to a relationship. Like today's 'spirituality', the idols of the ancient world were the products of human introspection. But God is personal and Other, no mere projection of our own preferences. He alone is real and can bear the weight of human identity. To settle for less is to chase a reflection of our own selves.

Monotheism – fidelity to the one God – is to religion what monogamy is to human relationships. The natural human impulse, particularly in a consumer society, is to keep all options open. But the paradox is that it is only when we finally choose to shut down all other options that we discover the truth: Christian monotheism produces good worship, just as monogamy produces good sex. It is the expression of a relationship of complete trust with one who is Other than myself. Consumer 'spirituality', like sexual promiscuity, condemns a person to perpetual frustration, because he is never able to climb out of his own head long enough to experience the wonder of real encounter.

THE DISTORTED SELF

Faithful encounter is much harder than promiscuous self-centredness, for the simple reason that encounter, with the true God or with another person, involves a living subject, and not a passive object for my personal pleasure. And this opens me up to something most of us find very difficult: being shown where we are in the wrong.

This is not a hazard encountered in contemporary spirituality, because there the self is never wrong. As the curates of our own souls, Moore says the sign of the soulful life is that we know and accept ourselves (xvii). Any sign of self-criticism is a sign of a personality which is not integrated, which has failed to honour its 'shadow' or darker side. Even our tendency towards violence is to be encouraged as an example of our own life-force: 'There is nothing neutral about the soul. It is the seat and the source of life. Either we respond to what the soul presents in its fantasies and desires, or we suffer from the neglect of ourselves' (129).

It seems to me extraordinary that when critics of Christianity attack it, their first target is the part of Christianity which is self-evidently true: its doctrine of sin. When I was in my early twenties, I spent some time reassessing my religious faith. For a while belief in God seemed impossible and I had no choice but to see myself as an atheist. But even in my time of deepest questioning, I never doubted Christianity's claim that there is something fundamentally wrong with the human heart. Malcolm Muggeridge wrote that the only part of Christianity which can be demonstrated from the morning paper is its doctrine of original sin.

Generation X marks the end-point of the experiment of secular humanism. For decades our culture has worked on the assumption that human beings are naturally good, that our only hindrances are external, and as we pursue our personal freedom and 'self-realization' utopia will be just around the corner. And the result of our greater freedom and throwing off external hindrances has been unprecedented levels of divorce, unparalleled levels of addiction, and a lower level of psychic wellbeing than any society in history.

The Professor of Psychology at New York University, Paul Vitz, asks the question which fashionable me-ology is desperate to avoid: 'If people are so good, how did societies get so bad?'[6] His own conclusion is that the Christian doctrine of original sin contains the clue: there is a fundamental distortion in human nature. We need not so much self-realization as detoxification. Not individuation, but salvation.

Consumer spirituality is superficially appealing, but on closer inspection its deep-seated selfishness turns out to be part of the problem. Christian Spirituality seems initially harsh and demanding. But its demands are the demands of relationship with a person, a person who tells us the truth about ourselves – even the truth we do not like to hear. It is only when we admit we are sick, as individuals and society, that we begin to ask for healing.

The person who invites us into a relationship is not content to leave us preening ourselves in our gilded mirrors, but calls us to gritty realism in our self-assessment. He calls us to repentance and new birth. He calls us to wonder restored.

WONDER RESTORED

Generation X asks 'Who am I?' The shopping mall says: 'You are a consumer; buy an identity.' The humanist says: 'You are an individual; sort yourself out.' The bestselling writer on spirituality says: 'You are in need of self-realization; go deeper within.' The Xer replies: 'I have bought so many identities I no longer have a clue who I am. I participate in a culture of self-ishness so screwed up that I can do nothing to change my world. I have gone deeper within and found only emptiness. My inheritance is to be a person of no fixed identity in a world with no wonder.'

God says: you are a person made in my image. You are made for intimacy with me and with others, to care for my earth and develop its potential. Your inheritance is to have a stable identity, in a world charged up with glory. Be reborn into wonder.

The small child looks at the universe with wide-eyed wonder. It is a world where even the oldest things become new, because the child is looking at them through his own new eyes. The journalist who has just escaped a near-fatal car crash looks at the universe with wide-eyed wonder. It is a world where even

126

the familiar things become an astonishing gift, because that journalist looks at them with a new gratitude.

It is puzzling that the Christian Church is so defensive and self-conscious about the one unique thing it has to offer the world: a promise of rebirth. All the consumer spirituality, all the humanist psychology, all the paganism in the world does not possess what one tacky mission tent, a wobbly organ and a preacher in a bad suit can possess: the key to wonder restored, death to selfishness and a world screwed up by human sin, rebirth into newness, intimacy with God and each other, rebirth to a vision of an earth renewed in glory. It is a hope of freshness and wonder which a whole generation longs to hear.

APPENDIX

TWELVE THINGS TO REMIND YOU THAT THE WORLD IS A WONDERFUL PLACE

1 Sunny conservatories filled with plants.

2 Babies' smiles.

3 Old maps of the world.

4 Mexican taco salad.

5 Cold mountain streams.

6 Making up after an argument.

7 Rivers in the middle of cities.

8 English pubs with log fires.

9 Good friends.

10 Springtime.

11 Seedless grapes.

12 God so loved the world that he gave his one and only Son, that whoever believes in him shall not perish but have eternal life.

TWELVE WAYS TO HELP RESTORE
LOST WONDER

1 Take a toddler to the zoo.

2 Start reading poetry.

3 Give your favourite person a list of
the ten things you like best about them.

4 Read a different paper/retune to a
different radio station.

5 Try a new, daring hairstyle.

6 Fly a kite.

7 Stop watching TV for a month.

8 Surprise somebody close to you with
a gratuitous act of wild generosity.

9 Read one of the four Gospels straight through.

10 Buy a new bike and ride it often.

11 Put on your favourite music and dance around
the room. Preferably with small children.

12 Take up gardening.

NOTES

INTRODUCTION

1. G.K. Chesterton, *Autobiography* (1936). In *Collected Works of G.K. Chesterton* (Ignatius Press 1988), Vol. XVI, p. 96.
2. Conversation with a friend. Quoted in M. Ward, *Gilbert Keith Chesterton* (Sheed & Ward 1945), p. 45.
3. G.K. Chesterton, *Homesick at Home* (1896). In *Collected Works of G.K. Chesterton* (Ignatius Press 1993), Vol. XIV, p. 64.
4. G.K. Chesterton, *Heretics* (1905). In *Collected Works of G.K. Chesterton* (Ignatius Press 1986) Vol. I, p. 55.

CHAPTER 1

1. C. Trungpa, *The Development of Ego*. In S. Bercholz, and S. Chödzin Kohn, (eds), *Entering the Stream: An Introduction to the Buddha and his Teachings* (Rider Books 1994), p. 76.

CHAPTER 2

1. M. Mahedy and J. Bernardi, *A Generation Alone* (IVP USA 1994), p. 75.
2. See M. Starkey, *Fashion & Style* (Monarch 1995).
3. Quoted in *New Trends for Youth Workers* (Australia), Vol. 1, 1995, p. 3.
4. *New Trends*, p. 3.

CHAPTER 3

1. R. Rolheiser, *Forgotten Among the Lilies: Learning to Live Beyond Our Own Obsessions* (Spire 1990), p. 35.

CHAPTER 4

1. M. Mason, *The Mystery of Marriage* (Multnomah/MARC Europe 1985), p. 27.
2. *Mystery of Marriage*, p. 117.
3. R. Michael, J. Gagnon, E. Laumann, and G. Kolata, *Sex in America: A Definitive Survey* (Little, Brown & Co 1994).
4. See L. Ryken, *Worldly Saints: The Puritans as They Really Were* (Zondervan 1986), p. 39.
5. D. Delvin and C. Webber, *The Big 'O': Understanding and Improving Your Orgasm* (New English Library 1995), p. 207.
6. T. Campolo, *Who Switched the Price Tags? A Search for Values in a Mixed-Up World* (Word 1986), p. 149.
7. E. Wheat, *Love Life for Every Married Couple* (Marshall Pickering 1984) is slightly old-fashioned in tone, but contains helpful suggestions for kindling or rekindling love in a relationship.
8. S. Arterburn, *Addicted to 'Love'* (Eagle 1991) is a good Christian analysis of unhelpful and destructive addictions to romantic and sexual fantasy.

CHAPTER 5

1. S. Hoggart, *America: A User's Guide* (Collins 1990), p. 111.
2. D. Burnett, *Dawning of the Pagan Moon* (Monarch 1991), p. 200.
3. For more on this idea of ancient paganism as a kind of poetic, prophetic foreshadowing – of which Christianity is the concrete fulfilment – see G.K. Chesterton, *The Everlasting Man* (1925), in *Collected Works of G.K. Chesterton* (Ignatius Press 1986), Vol. II, especially Chapter V, 'Man and Mythologies'; and C.S. Lewis, *Surprised by Joy* (Fontana, 1959), especially Chapter XV, 'The Beginning'.
4. Starhawk, *Truth or Dare: Encounters with Power, Authority, and Mystery* (Harper & Row 1987), pp. 4, 6.
5. See A.B. Spencer, (ed.), *The Goddess Revival* (Baker 1995), p. 106. A good analysis of the goddess movement with a helpful Christian response.

CHAPTER 6

1. See M. Starkey, *Born to Shop* (Monarch 1989).
2. T. Moore, *Care of the Soul* (HarperCollins 1992).
3. D. Wells, *God in the Wasteland* (Eerdmans/IVP 1994), chapter 5.
4. C.S. Lewis, *Miracles* (Fontana 1960), p. 98.
5. A. Dillard, The Annie Dillard Reader (HarperCollins 1994), p. 38.
6. P. Vitz, *Psychology as Religion: The Cult of Self-Worship* (2nd edn), (Eerdmans/Paternoster 1994), p. 43.